The Village Atlas

The Growth of Manchester,
Lancashire & North Cheshire,
1840 - 1912

The Village Atlas

The Growth of Manchester,
Lancashire & North Cheshire,
1840 - 1912

The Alderman Press

Published by The Village Press Limited
7d Keats Parade, Church Street, Edmonton, N9 9DP.

October 1989.

The Village Press 1989

British Library Cataloguing in Publication Data

The village atlas : the growth of Manchester-Lancashire & North Cheshire, 1840-1912.

  1. Metropolitan County, Greater Manchester, history, maps, atlases
  I. Bruff, Barry Robson, 1926-
  912'. 4273

ISBN 0-946619-34-4

Typesetting by Stone Associates, Winchmore Hill.
Artwork by Active Arts, Winchmore Hill.
Printed and bound in Gt. Britain
by The Bath Press, Bath, Avon.

Acknowledgements.

The publishers would like to thank the staff of the Map Library and Photographic Department of the
British Library for their help during the preparation of this Atlas.

The staff of the local History Department of Manchester Central Library.

The staff of the Reference Library, Enfield, Middlesex.

Introduction

The nineteenth century was one of unparalleled growth in population and cities. The Industrial Revolution drew people to the large urban centres like a magnet and housing and factories to accommodate them grew accordingly. Lancashire, one of the most industrialised counties of England, more than most.

Manchester, its chief town, like Birmingham an important communication centre, with its position astride major road networks, was the attraction for industry and therefore people.

Development and, in a very short space of time, redevelopment took place along the arterial roads. Villages and small market towns along the way, which for centuries had had their own independent life and local government, found themselves engulfed in a tide of bricks and mortar, seemingly overnight. Anyone who lived in the centre of Manchester in 1800 would have had only a short walk to the countryside. They would have had a journey of several miles by the end of the century, should they have lived so long.

Industry thrived where there were good communications and the canal system provided reasonably quick (for the times) transport of goods in bulk. It was the appearance of the railways and steam power that produced the final impetus for industry of the time. To Manchester, of course, goes the honour of being chosen by Stephenson for the first demonstration of his "Rocket", which ran along a section of the Liverpool-Manchester Railway in 1829 at a speed of 30 m.p.h. This pioneer railway which opened in 1830 had its terminus at Campfield. London Road station opened in 1841.Two stations, Exchange and Victoria opened in 1844 and Central Station in 1877.

There were other reasons for the growth in population. Public health, very bad perhaps by our standards, was nevertheless vastly improved during the century. For example, although the population of Blackburn showed considerable growth during the century, the increase shown in census figures in 1821 was 13,500, which was perhaps double what might have been expected. This was put down to the introduction of vaccination.

As elsewhere, development closely followed the railway, especially when suburban stations were opened, usually accompanied by a "Railway Hotel" and adjacent shops.

The centre of Manchester saw many changes during the century due to the widening and straightening of its ancient streets. Hunts Bank was opened out in 1833. Corporation Street was formed about 1850. In 1869 more improvements were made. Several narrow, old lanes were done away with including the old Smithy Door, bringing about the formation of Deansgate and Victoria Street.

Manchester increased in size and importance, the Town Hall was built 1822-5 and in 1832 Manchester became a parliamentary borough. As in other places, outlying townships had now become an indistinguishable part of the city and as well as Manchester Town the new borough included **Hulme, Chorlton-upon-Medlock, Ardwick, Beswick and Cheetham**. Manchester became a city in 1853 and a county borough in 1888. The population of Manchester, 70,469 in 1801, had increased to 303,382 by 1851, however, that of the inner city actually decreased as people moved to the suburbs due to the construction of the roads and railways. By 1901 the population of the city with its much changed boundaries was 543,872.

Beswick. Population 96 in 1801 and still only 881 in 1861 was 11,516 in 1901. Likewise, Bradford Township, 94 in 1801 was 23,427 in 1901, so that Manchester Town had a population of 426,944 in 1901.

Chorlton-upon-Medlock, one of the older parts of the city, had a population of 675 in 1801 which increased to 2581 by 1811; 8209 by 1821; 20,569 by 1831; 28,336 by 1841; 35,558 by 1851; 44,795 by 1861, rising to a peak of 59,645 by 1891, then showing a decline to 57,953 by 1901, probably due to public building and redevelopment.

Cheetham, an ancient township grew from a population of 767 in 1801 to 37,947 by 1901. Industries here included breweries and chemical dye works.

Crumpsall, where cotton mills, print, bleach and dye works had been built by 1852, increased from 425 in 1801 to nearly 12,000 in 1901.

Harperhey, is described in the Lancashire Gazetteer 1830 as "abounding in pleasant views". Cotton printing had begun here in 1788 and by 1833 there were spinning mills, engineering and print works. It became part of Manchester in 1896. The tiny population of 118 in 1801 had increase to 15,489 by 1901.

Newton became part of Manchester in 1896 and was very much affected by railway building. It was crossed by the Lancashire and Yorkshire Railway and several other lines with extensive goods yards. The Rochdale Grand Canal also passed through it. These together assured its rapid industrialisation and development. The population had reached 11,000 by the middle of the century and 40,533 by 1901.

Failsworth is also crossed by railways and canals. It had old industries of hat making and silk weaving but its growth was mainly due to cotton spinning. It already had a population of 2622 in 1801 but probably due to its mainly industrial development, it had only risen to 14,152 by the end of the century.

Blackley, the northernmost part of the parish became part of the city in 1890. In 1850 there was an old water corn mill which was also used for grinding log wood. Population had only reached 9012 by 1901 as this was one of the later parts of Manchester to be developed, although by 1900 there was a certain amount of industry including a chemical works.

The district of **Bradford** covered only 288 acres but the industries included iron and chemical works. Mostly residential, as shown in the rise of population from a mere 165 in 1831 to 23,427 in 1901.

Population figures are sometimes a little misleading as there are sometimes variations which occur that are nothing to do with natural increase. An instance of this is in Chorley, now an important town to the North-West of Manchester. In 1841 the population shot up to 13,149 from 9282 in 1831. The rise was due to the presence of labourers employed on the Bolton and Preston Railway.

Ardwick. Many railways crossed the borough. The London and North Western, The Lancashire and Yorkshire; the Great Central Company had a line which ran parallel with the Lancashire and Yorkshire and connected with the Midland Railway and this, together with Ancoats Goods Station brought industry to the area, india-rubber, dye works, saw mills, boiler works and pottery among them. It had the highest population of any of the original boroughs in 1832. 1,762 in 1801, 15,777 in 1851, rising to 40,847 in 1901.

Droylesden had both railways and canals running round and through it bringing many industries. Cotton and linen weaving had been established for many years but during the nineteenth century, many associated industries flourished including chemicals, an iron foundry, printing and brick-making. Population figures rose from 1532 in 1801 to nearly 20,000 in 1901.

Openshaw developed like a finger from the city centre, stretching two miles along the main road to Ashton and became part of the city in 1890. The population, 339 in 1801 rose to 26,690 by 1901.

Withington. Development here extended ribbon-wise along the road to Northenden in Cheshire and was mainly urban in character having two stations which encouraged most of the building in the latter half of the century. There were only 2,712 people in 1861 living in an area of 250 acres but by 1901 the figure had risen to 20,022.

Didsbury. Here again building occurred late in the century, mainly after 1861. It also had two stations one of which was Didsbury which opened in 1875. Population increased from 1,829 in 1861 to 9,988 by 1901.

Chorlton-with-Hardy or Chorlton-cum-Hardy had a very similar pattern of growth to Didsbury, 513 in 1801 but not really growing at all until the 1860's. Population was only 731 in 1861 but then it grew rapidly, reaching 9,026 in 1901.

Moss Side has long been an indistinguishable part of Manchester but here again the main growth was in the latter half of the century. A small township of 150 people in 1801, it more than tripled in size from 2,695 to 8,403 between 1861 and 1871, then escalated over the next thirty years to 26,583 in 1901.

Levenshulme. The western half of the township became a residential suburb but the eastern half was heavily industrialised with print, bleach and dye works associated with the all-important cotton industry. Population was only 628 in 1801 but had reached 11,485 in 1901.

Burnage. Described not so long ago as a rural township, it had a population of 1,888 in 1901. What development there was in the 1800's, took place in the last twenty years of the century.

Denton, long famous for its hat trade, surprisingly had a population of 1,362 in 1801 but had only reached 9,988 in 1901, having increased steadily throughout the century.

Heaton Norris, considering its distance from the city centre, also had a comparatively large population in 1801 of 3,768 and it also showed a very steady increase over the years, until in 1901 it had reached 26,540. The fact that it was served by several railway companies, probably had a great deal to do with its development.

Reddish. In the 1850's, a population of around 1,200 lived in the small town of Reddish and the hamlets of Reddish Green, Sandford, and Whitehill. The road to Stockport passed through the village of South Reddish. In 1857 there was not even a post office, schoolmaster or doctor. Interestingly it was noted that there was no pawnbroker either. Later, however, there were cotton mills and calico printing works. Population in 1901 was 8,668.

Stretford, with 3,255 acres, was one of the largest boroughs of Manchester. The main road followed the line of the Roman road to Chester. Growth was slow until the middle of the century, from whence it grew in leaps and bounds reaching 30,436 by 1901.

On its northern boundaries, on the River Irwell, are the docks and jetties of the Ship Canal. The American Civil War had a disastrous effect on Lancashire due to the embargo on cotton and there was a general decline in trade which was only finally reversed by the opening of the Manchester Ship Canal. Carrying ocean-going vessels direct from Eastham on the Mersey it was begun in 1887 and opened in 1894. In a century of engineering marvels the Ship Canal certainly ranks among the greatest.

Hulme, one of the original districts making up the parliamentary borough in 1832. Its situation inevitably meant early development. On the line of the Roman road to Chester, it already had a population of nearly 27,000 in 1841, then there was an amazing ten years when it virtually doubled, after which there was steady growth until it reached 66,916 in

1901. The fact that the Birmingham Canal had its terminus here with quays, warehouses and docks, with all their attendant industries and several railways, all contributed to its tremendous growth.

Liverpool, the second largest city of Lancashire and the gateway for Lancashire's trade with the world particularly North and South America. Its first dock opened in 1751 but in the nineteenth century, apart from a hiatus during the American Civil War, its pattern of growth followed the other great cities. Together with Toxteth, Walton, Everton, Kirkdale and West Derby the population had risen by 1901 to approximately 850,000 from 87,878 in 1901. In 1830 the city covered 1,860 acres but with the acquisition of Walton, West Derby, Wavertree and the southern half of Toxteth, at the end of the century it had risen to 16,619 acres.

In the eighteen months following 1845-6, the years of the potato famine in Ireland, the population was swelled by an influx of Irish immigrants numbering some 400,000. Most of these subsequently went to America but many remained to add to the growth of Liverpool.

Many other towns of Lancashire and Cheshire also showed considerable growth, not necessarily industrial, as a glance at the maps will show and some comparative figures may be helpful.

	1801	1851	1901
BLACKBURN	33,631	84,919	506,291
BURNLEY	3,305	141,706	44,045
BURY	21,161	66,761	98,297
LANCASTER	9,030	14,378	31,224
LYTHAM	920	2,698	13,992
OLDHAM	12,024	52,820	137,246
PRESTON	14,300	72,136	115,483
ROCHDALE	29,092	80,214	140,545
STOCKPORT	28,344	91,423	78,871
WARRINGTON	13,180	26,651	62,041
WIDNES	1,063	3,217	28,580
WIGAN	13,310	28,068	88,763

This introduction is only intended as the merest outline of the story of the growth of Lancashire and North Cheshire and I apologise in advance for any omissions but hope the maps will speak for themselves.

Barry Bruff
London, 1989.

BIBLIOGRAPHY

The Victoria History of the Counties of England.
Editor: Christopher Elrington. Publishers: Oxford
University Press.

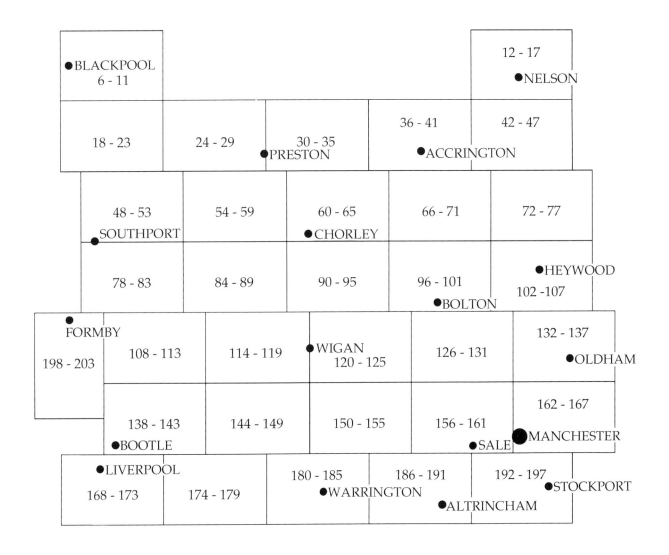

The Maps

Publisher's Note

The maps in this Atlas are based on a scale of two inches to the mile. However, because of the number of different maps involved and the reproduction thereof there may be some minor variations in scale. The age of the maps and the fact that there could be as much as fifteen years difference between the dates of survey of adjoining maps, plus the handling and folding which has taken place over the years, have also meant that there are small differences here and there which are impossible to eradicate.

The publishers have made every effort to minimise these faults and trust the reader will make allowances for any slight imperfections.

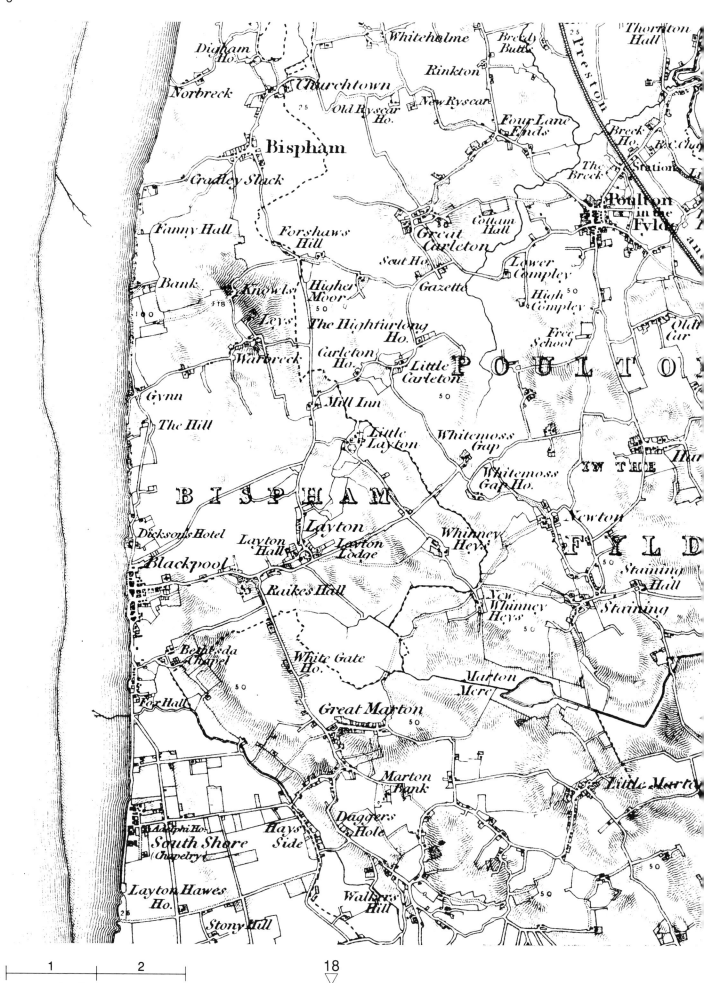

Digham Ho.
Whitcholme
Brecb Butts
Thornton Hall
Churchtown
Rinkton
Norbreck
Old Ryscar Ho.
New Ryscar
Four Lane Ends
Breck Ho.
Bacchus
Bispham
The Breck
Poulton in the Fyle
Cradley Slack
Great Carleton
Cottam Hall
Forshaws Hill
Fanny Hall
Lower Com/ley
Scut Ho.
Bank
Knowls'
Higher Moor
Gazette
High Comley
Leys
Free School
Oldt Car
The Highfurlong Ho.
POULTO
Warbreck
Carleton Ho.
Gynn
Mill Inn
Little Carleton
50
The Hill
Little Layton
Whitemoss Gap
Whitemoss Gap Ho.
IN THE
BISPHAM
Newton
Dickson's Hotel
Layton
Layton Lodge
Whinney Heys
FYLD
Blackpool
Layton Hall
Staining Hall
Raikes Hall
New Whinney Heys
Staining
Bethesda Chapel
White Gate Ho.
50
Marton Mere
Fox Hall
Great Marton
50
Marton Bank
Little Marton
Adelphi Ho.
Hays Side
Daggers Hole
South Shore (Chapelry)
Layton Hawes Ho.
Walkers Hill
50
Stony Hill

1   2
1 mile approx.

18
▽

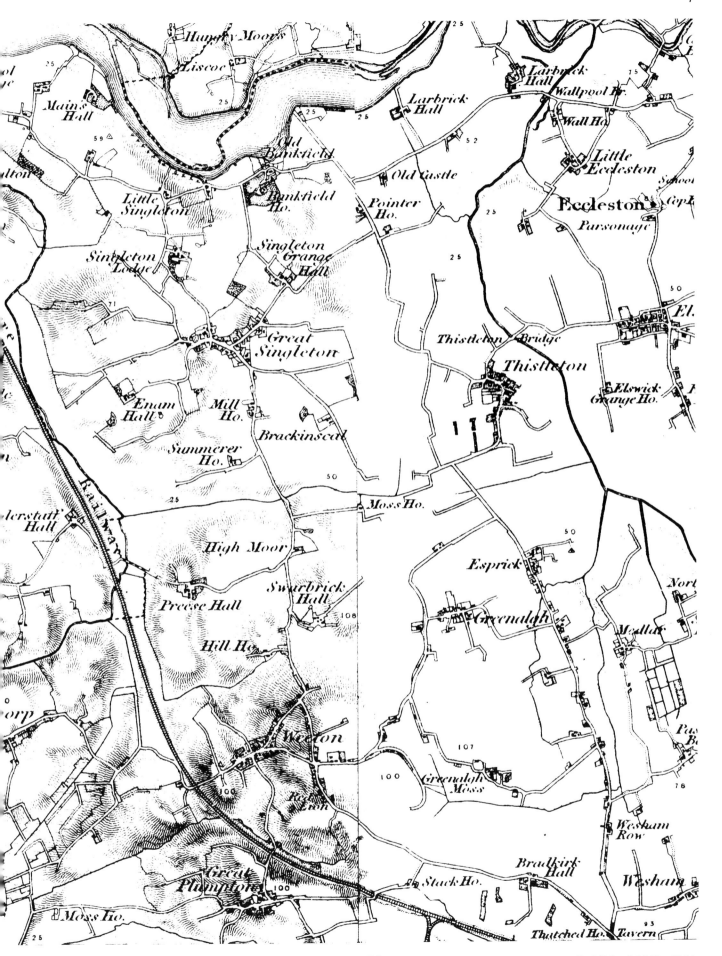

Published 1840 - 1844.

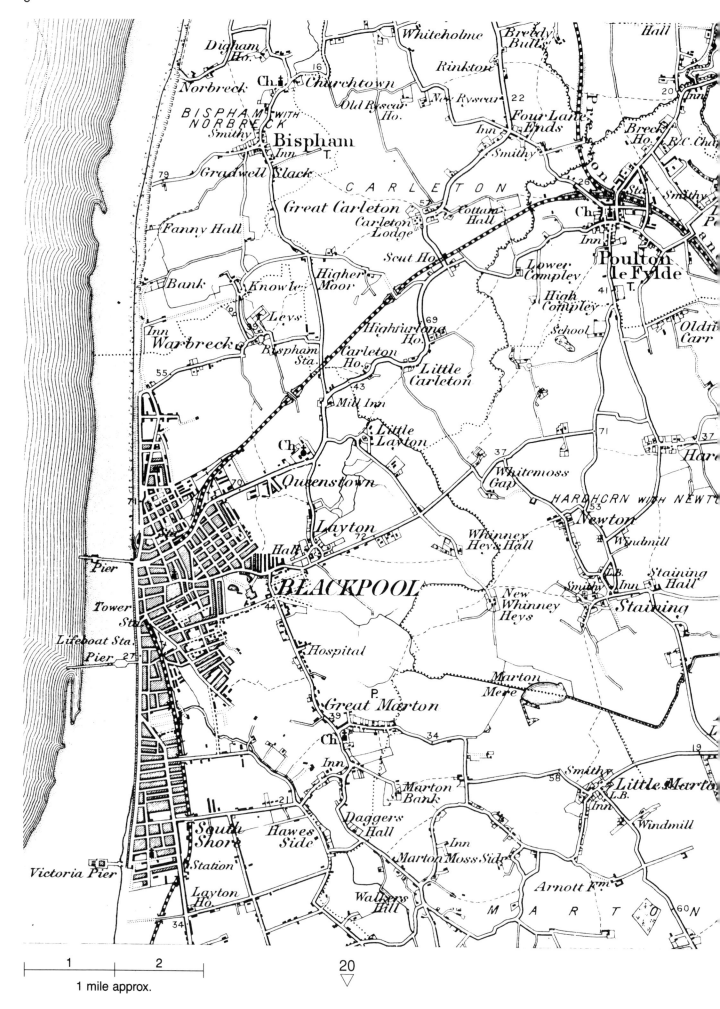

Digham Ho.
Whiteholme
Bredy Bulls
Hall
Norbreck
Ch.
Churchtown
Rinkton
BISPHAM WITH NORBRECK
Smithy
Old Ryscar Ho.
New Ryscar
22
Four Lane Ends
Breck Ho.
R.C.Ch.
Bispham
Inn
T.
Smithy
Sta.
Smithy
Gradwell Slack
CARLETON
26
79
Great Carleton
57
Cottam Hall
Ch.
Poulton le Fylde
Carleton Lodge
Lower Complex
Inn
Fanny Hall
Scut Ho.
High Complex
41
T.
Bank
Higher Moor
School
Oldm Carr
Knowle
Levs
High Furlong Ho.
69
Inn
Warbreck
Bispham Sta.
Carleton Ho.
Little Carleton
Hare
55
71
37
43
Mill Inn
Whitemoss Gap
37
HARDHORN WITH NEWT
Ch.
Little Layton
53
Queenstown
Newton
Windmill
Layton
72
Whinney Heys Hall
Staining Hall
Hall
L.B.
Smithy
Inn
BLACKPOOL
New Whinney Heys
Staining
Pier
44
Tower
Sta.
Lifeboat Sta.
Pier
27
Hospital
Marton Mere
Marton Mere
P.
Great Marton
39
34
19
Victoria Pier
Smithy
58
Little Marto
L.B.
Inn
21
Windmill
Daggers Hall
South Shore
Hawes Side
Marton Bank
Station
Inn
Marton Moss Side
Layton Ho.
MART O
Walters Hill
Arnott Fm
34
60 N

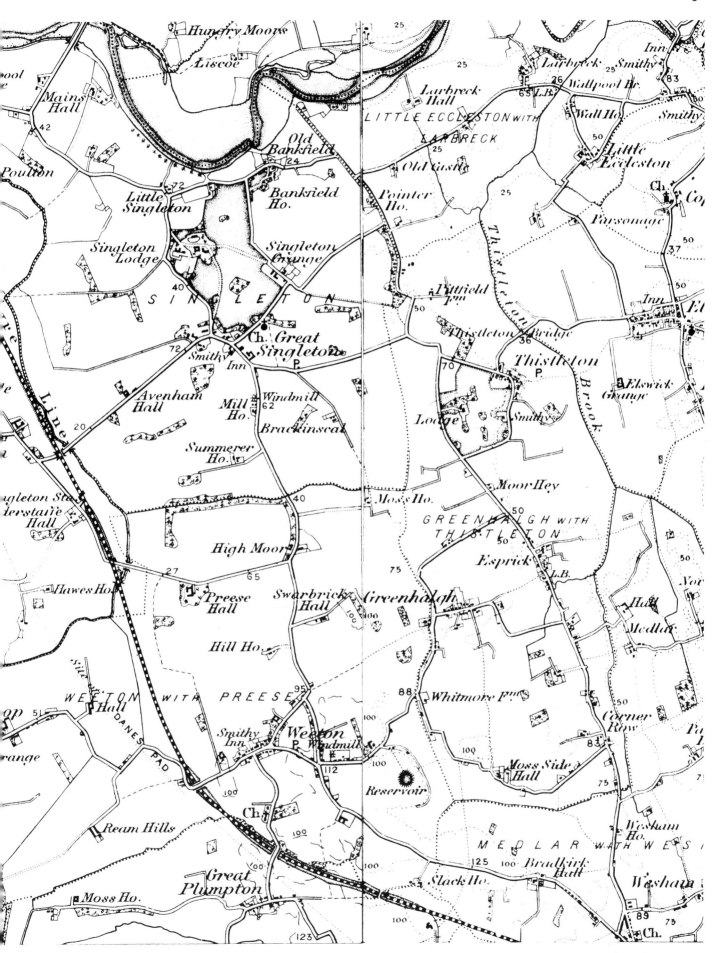

Hungry Moors

Liscoe

Mains Hall

Poulton

Little Singleton

Old Bankfield

Bankfield Ho.

Singleton Lodge

Singleton Grange

S I N G L E T O N

Ch. Great Singleton

Smithy

Inn

Avenham Hall

Mill Ho.

Windmill

Brackinscat

Summerer Ho.

Line

ngleton Sta.
erstaffe Hall

High Moor

Hawes Ho.

Preese Hall

Swarbrick Hall

Hill Ho.

W E E T O N W I T H P R E E S E

Hall

S I L D A N E S P A D

Weeton

Smithy Inn

Windmill

Reservoir

Ch.

Ream Hills

range

Moss Ho.

Great Plumpton

LITTLE ECCLESTON WITH
LARBRECK

Larbreck Hall

Old Castle

Pointer Ho.

Pittfield Fm.

Thistleton

Thistleton Bridge

Thistleton

Lodge

Smithy

Moor Hey

Moss Ho.

G R E E N H A L G H WITH
T H I S T L E T O N

Esprick

L.B.

Greenhalgh

Whitmore Fm.

Moss Side Hall

Bradkirk Halt

Slack Ho.

M E D L A R W I T H W E S

Larbreck

Smithy

Wallpool Br.

L.B.

Wall Ho.

Smithy

Little Eccleston

Ch.

Co

Parsonage

Inn

Elswick Grange

Medla

Hall

Nor

Corner Row

Wesham Ho.

Wesham

Ch.

Surveyed 1842 - 48. Revised 1896. Published 1897 - 98.

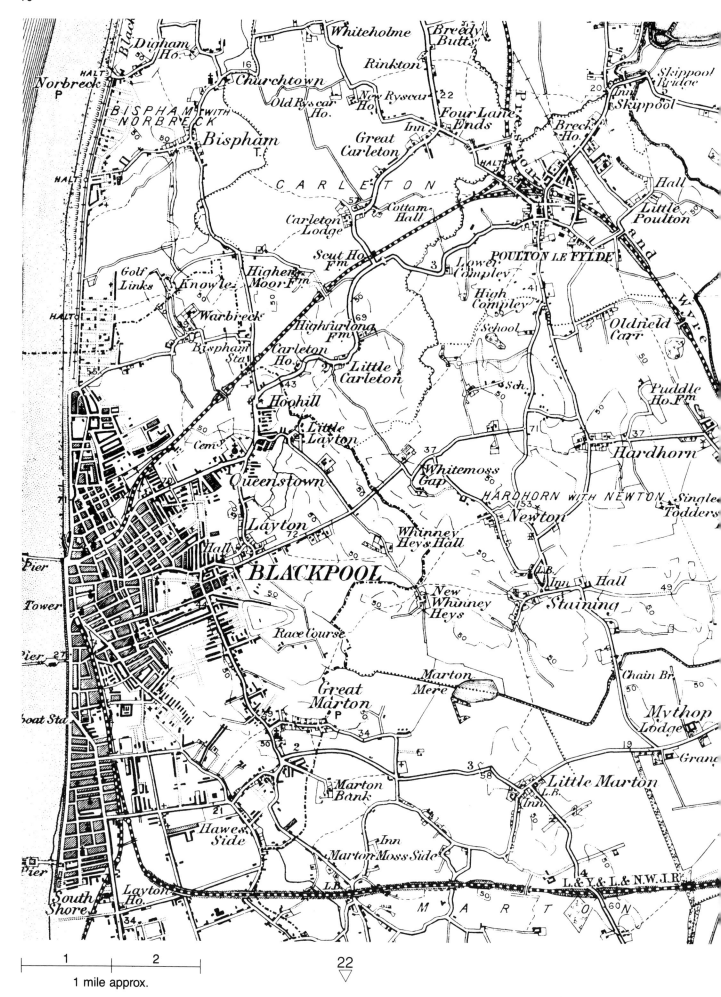

1 mile approx.

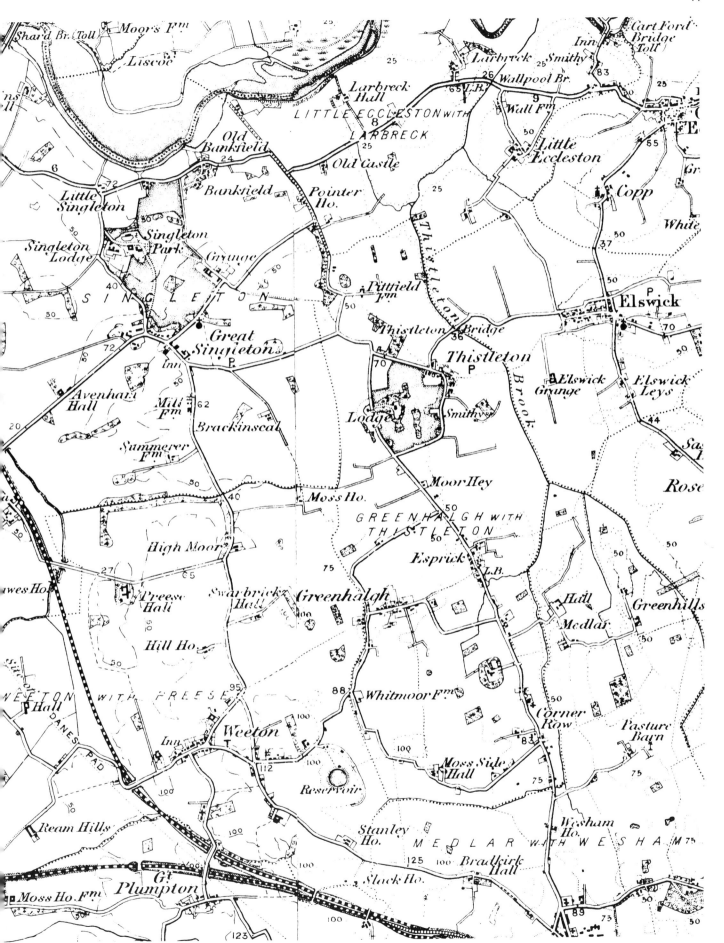

Shard Br. Toll   Moor's Fm   Liscoe

Larbreck   Smithy   Cart Ford Bridge Toll   Inn

Wallpool Br.   L.B.   Wall Fm

Larbreck Hall

LITTLE ECCLESTON WITH LARBRECK

Little Eccleston   Copp   White

Old Bankfield   Old Castle

Bankfield   Pointer Ho.

Little Singleton   Singleton Park   Grange

Singleton Lodge   Pitfield Fm   Elswick   P

S I N G L E T O N   Thistleton Bridge   Thistleton   P   Elswick Grange   Elswick Leys

Great Singleton   Inn   P   Lodge   Smithy   Sas

Avenham Hall   Mill Fm   Brackinscal   Moor Hey   Rose

Summerer Fm   Moss Ho.

GREENHALGH WITH THISTLETON

High Moor   Esprick   L.B.   Hall   Greenhills

Preese Hall   Swarbrick Hall   Greenhalgh   Medlar

Hill Ho.   Whitmoor Fm   Corner Row   Pasture Barn

W E E T O N   W I T H   F R E E S E   Hall   DANES PAD   Inn   Weeton   T   Moss Side Hall

Ream Hills   Reservoir   Stanley Ho.   Wesham Ho.   M E D L A R   W I T H   W E S H A M

Gt. Plumpton   Slack Ho.   Bradkirk Hall

Moss Ho. Fm

Surveyed 1842 - 48. Revised 1911 - 12. Published 1913.

1   2

1 mile approx.

42

Published 1840 - 1844.

1 mile approx.

44

Surveyed 1842 - 49. Revised 1896. Published 1898.

1 mile approx.

Surveyed 1842 - 49. Revised 1911. Published 1913.

6

Broad Lane

Milkers Gate Lane

Squires Lane

Midale Lane

Pony Hill

Blown Sands

Pewit Dubs

Hall Way Hou.
Black Leech
The Folds

Moss
House

Divisdale Lane

Marton

Mulge Land
Robin's Row

Moss

Old Hill

Fods

Division Lane

Moss
Edge

Leech Lane

Stair Lane Moss

Lytham

Lytham Moss

Widing Lane

Marton Lane

West
Moss

Grange

Dinery
Heights

West End

Head Room
Gate

Rve
Hey

Hey Houses

Wildings

Moss
Hall

North
Houses

Fancy
Lodge

Common Side Lane

South Houses

Hills

Landmark

Parsonage

The Wharf

Ly.

Town

Scar

1   2

1 mile approx.

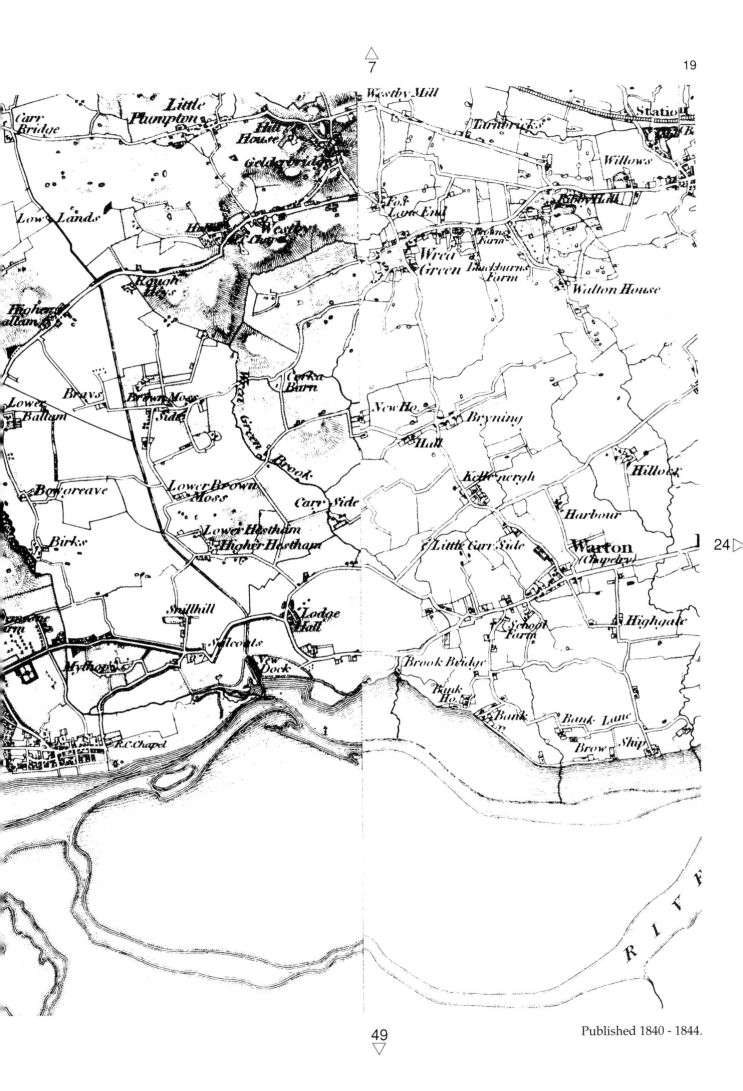

Carr
Bridge

Little
Plumpton

Hill
House

Geldgebridge

Low Lands

Rough
Moss

Higher
Ballam

Brays

Lower
Ballam

Brown Moss
Side

Bowgreave

Birks

Lower Brown
Moss

Snillhill

Mythops

R.C.Chapel

Salcoats

New
Dock

Lodge
Hall

Lower Hestham

Higher Hestham

Corka
Barn

Carr Side

Westby Mill

Tarnbricks

Willows

Fo.&
Lane End

Wrea
Green

Browns
Farm

Blackburns
Farm

Walton House

New Ho.

Bryning

Hall

Kellenergh

Harbour

Hillock

Little Carr Side

Warton
(Chapelry)

School
Farm

Brook Bridge

Bank
Ho.

Bank

Bank Lane

Brow Ship

Highgate

24 ▷

R I V E

Published 1840 - 1844.

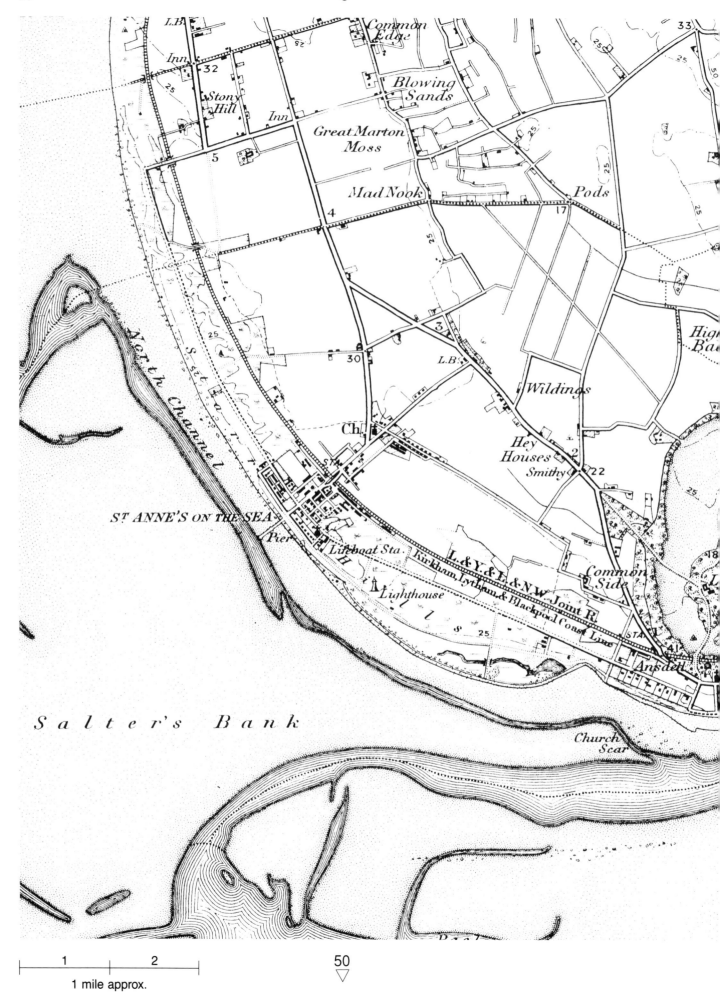

Common
Edge

L.B.

Inn

32

Stony
Hill

Inn

5

Blowing
Sands

Great Marton
Moss

Mad Nook

4

Pods

17

30

3

L.B.

Wildings

Ch.

Hey
Houses

2

Smithy

22

High
Ba

North Channel

St ANNE'S ON THE SEA

Pier

Lifeboat Sta.

Lighthouse

L. & Y. & L. & N.W. Joint R.

Kirkham, Lytham & Blackpool Coast Line

Common
Side

Ansdell

18

S a l t e r ' s   B a n k

Church
Scar

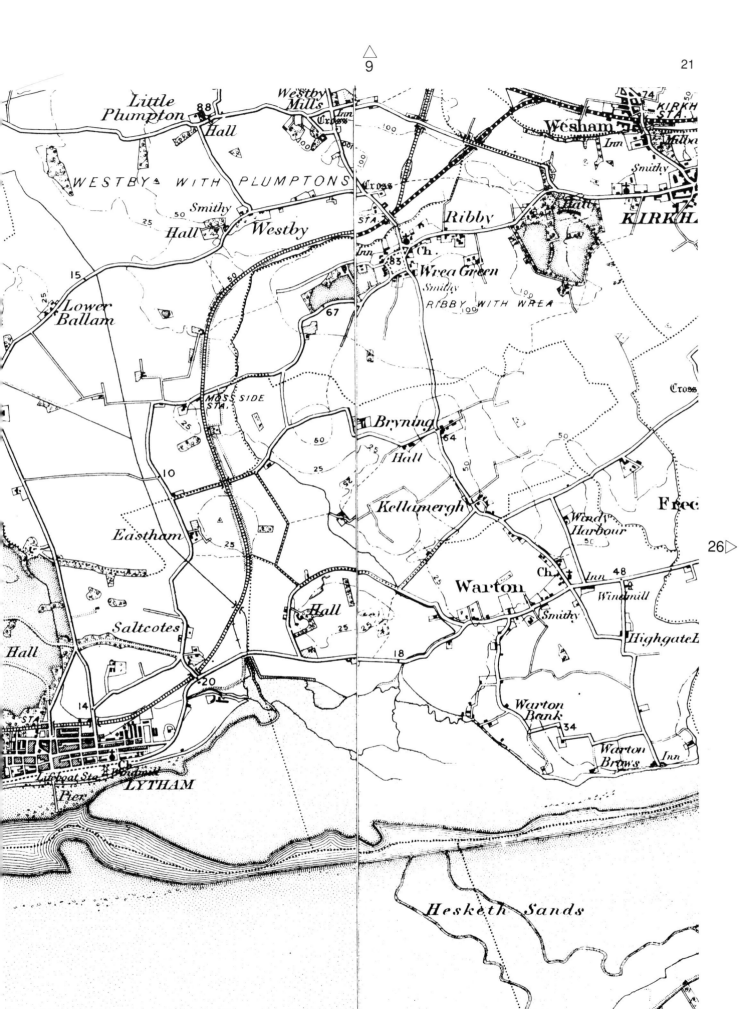

Little
Plumpton 88
Hall

Westby
Mills
Cross
Inn

Wesham

KIRKH
STA.

Inn
Millb

WESTBY WITH PLUMPTONS

Smithy
Smithy

Hall
Westby

KIRKH

Cross

Hall

STA.
Ribby

15

Inn
Ch.
83
Wrea Green

RIBBY WITH WREA

Smithy

100

Lower
Ballam

67

MOSS SIDE
STA.

50

Bryning

64

Hall

25

Eastham

Kellamergh

Windy
Harbour
50

Free

26 ▷

48

Warton

Ch.
Inn

Saltcotes

Hall

Smithy

Windmill

Highgate

18

Hall

STA.

14

20

Warton
Bank
34

Warton
Brows
Inn

Lifeboat Sta. Windmill
LYTHAM
Ch.

Pier

Hesketh Sands

Surveyed 1889 - 93. Revised 1895. Published 1896.

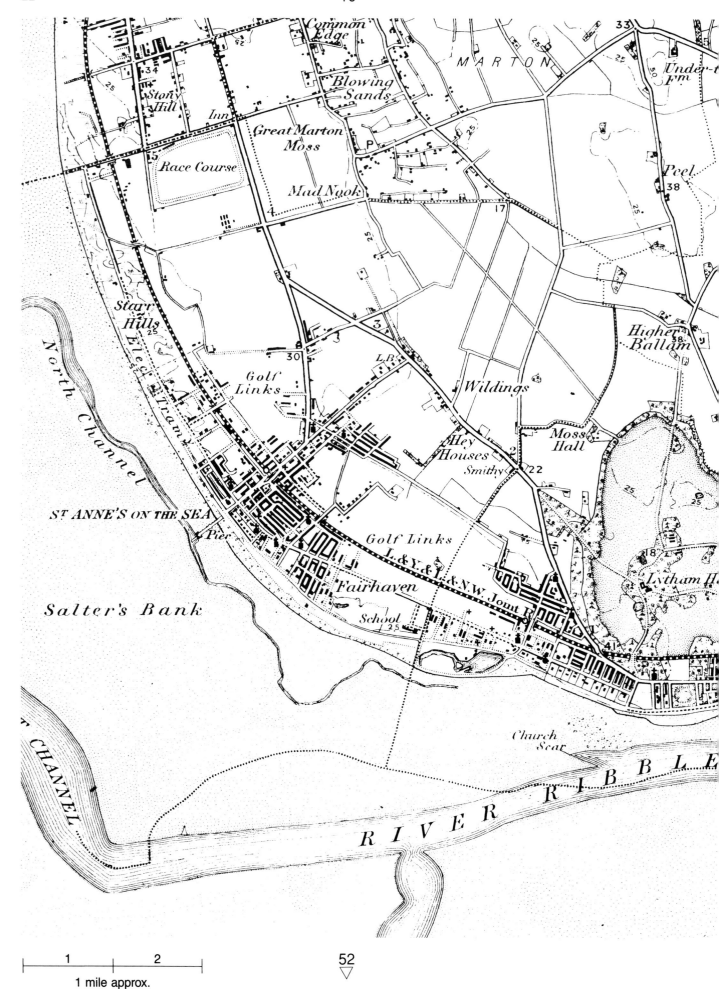

MARTON

33

Under-t
F'm

50

Common
Edge

Blowing
Sands

Stony
Hill

Inn

Peel
38

Great Marton
Moss

P

Race Course

25

Mad Nook

17

4

25

Starr
Hills

Higher
Ballam

3

30

Golf
Links

L.B.

Wildings

Moss
Hall

North Channel

Electr. Tram

Hey
Houses

2

22

Smithy

25

St ANNE'S ON THE SEA

25

Golf Links

Pier

L. & Y. & L. & N.W. Joint R.

Lytham H.

18

Fairhaven

School

25

Salter's Bank

41

Church
Scar

CHANNEL

RIVER RIBBLE

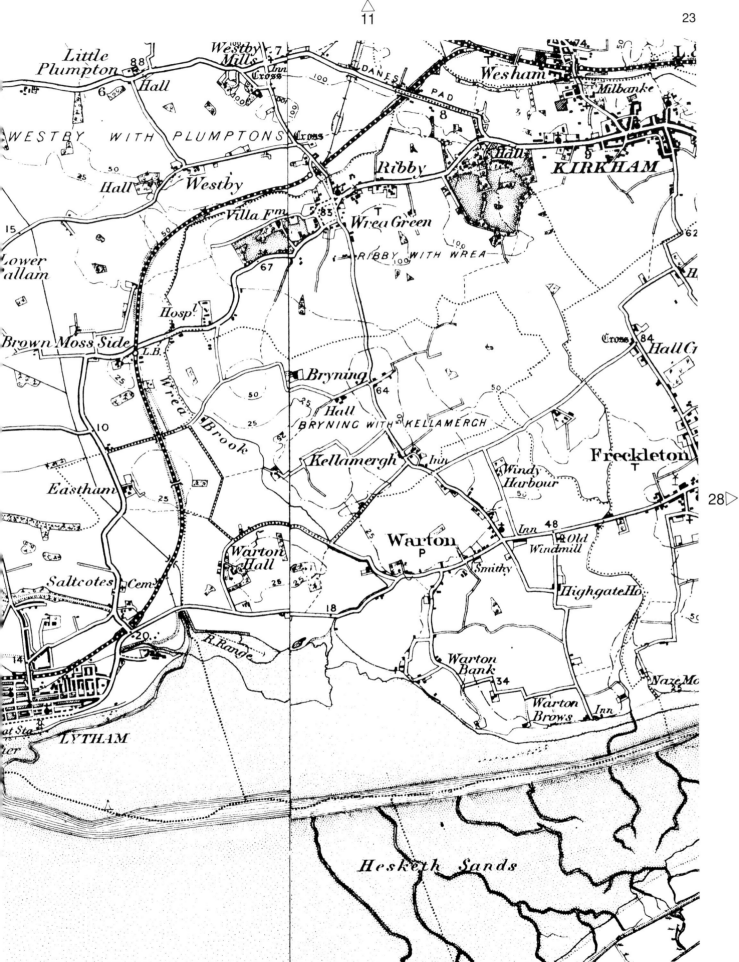

Surveyed 1842 - 44 / 1888 - 93. Revised 1912. Published 1913.

1	2

1 mile approx.

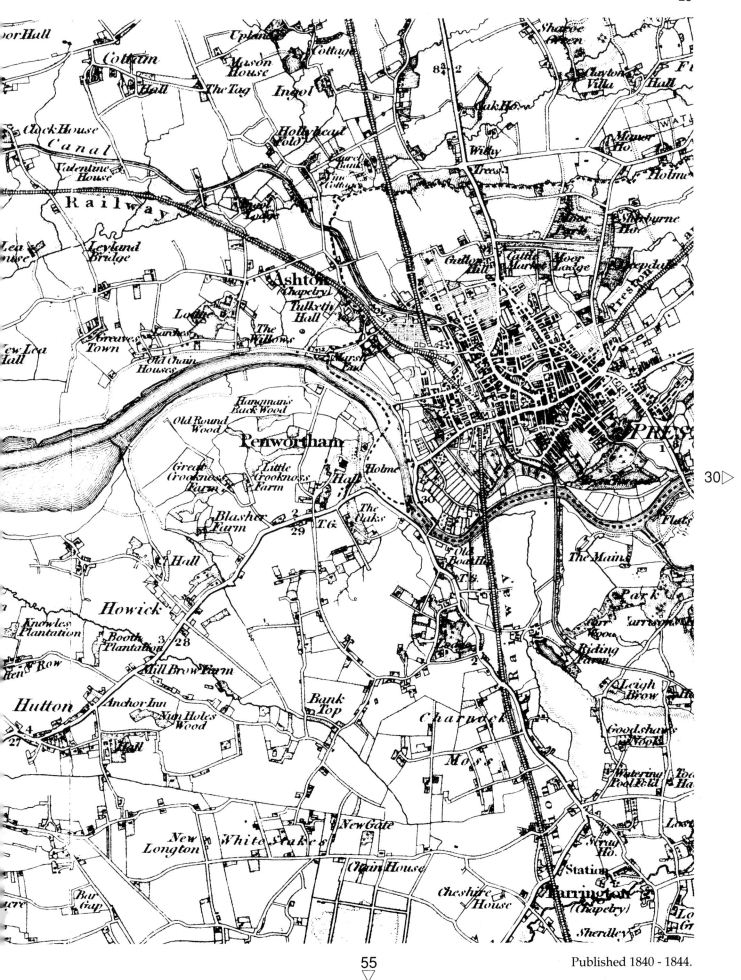

Published 1840 - 1844.

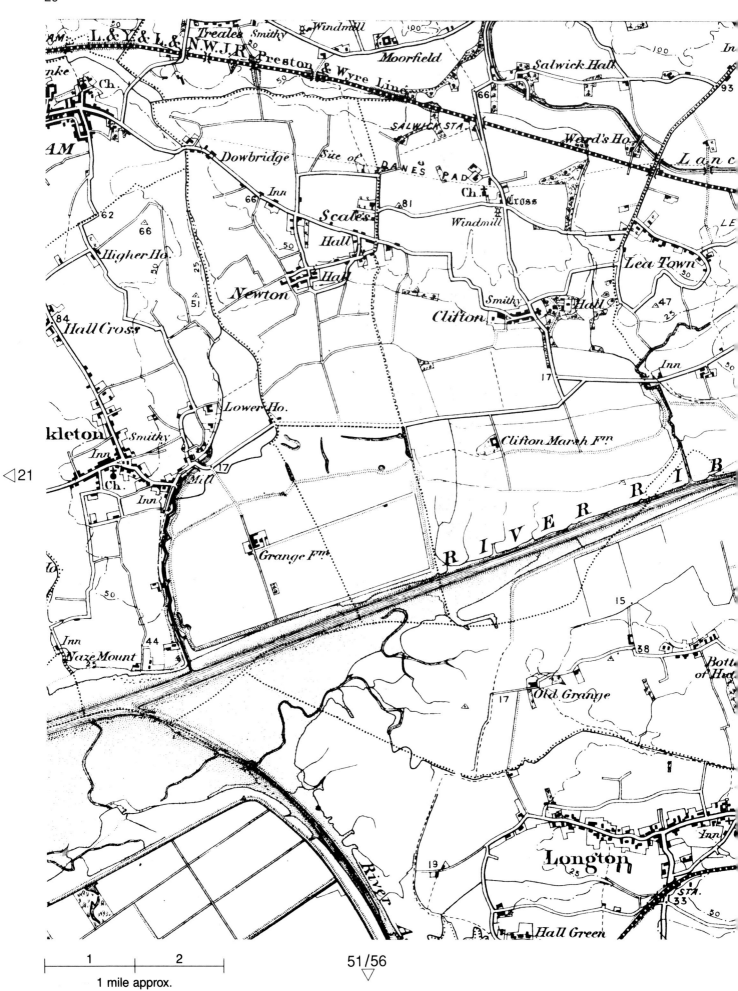

◁21

51/56
▽

1   2

1 mile approx.

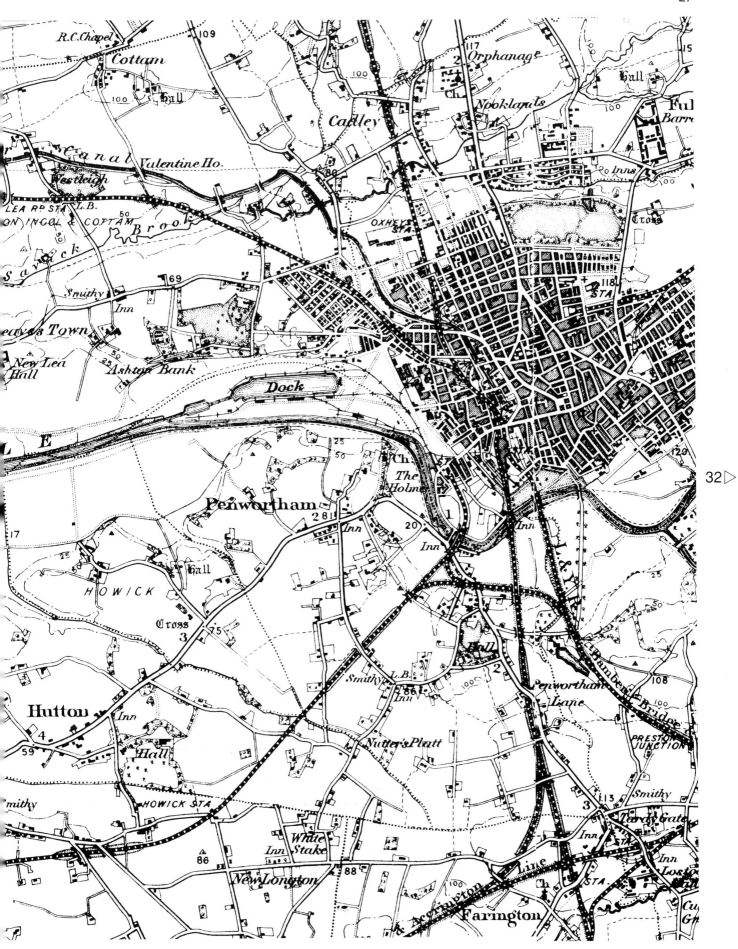

R.C.Chapel
Cottam
Hall
109
100
100
Catley
Orphanage
Nooklands
Hall
Ful
Barr
Canal
Valentine Ho.
Westleigh
Inns
LEA RD STA L.B.
ON INGOL & COTTAM
Brook
50
Cross
Savick
50
OXHEYS STA
69
Smithy
118 STA
Inn
eaves Town
New Lea Hall
Ashton Bank
25
50
Dock
25
129
25
50
Ch
The Holm
Penworth Bridge
Penwortham
281
Inn
20
1
Inn
17
Inn
Hall
HOWICK
25
Hall
Cross
3
75
2
108
Hutton
Inn
Smithy
L.B.
100
Inn
4
59
Hall
Nutter's Platt
100
PRESTON JUNCTION
smithy
113
Smithy
HOWICK STA
3
Tardy Gate
86
White Stake
Inn
Inn
Lost
Inn
New Longton
88
Accrington Line
Farington
Cu Gr

Surveyed 1889 - 93. Revised 1895. Published 1896.

32 ▷

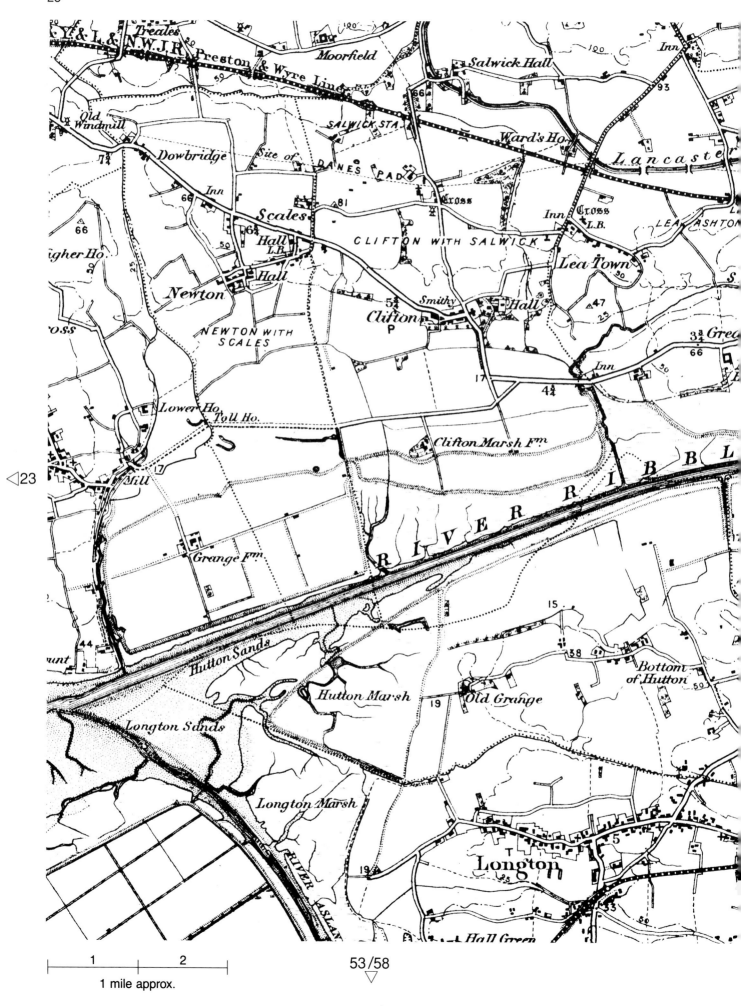

1 mile approx.

34 ▷

Surveyed 1842 - 44 / 1888 - 93. Revised 1912. Published 1913.

1 mile approx.

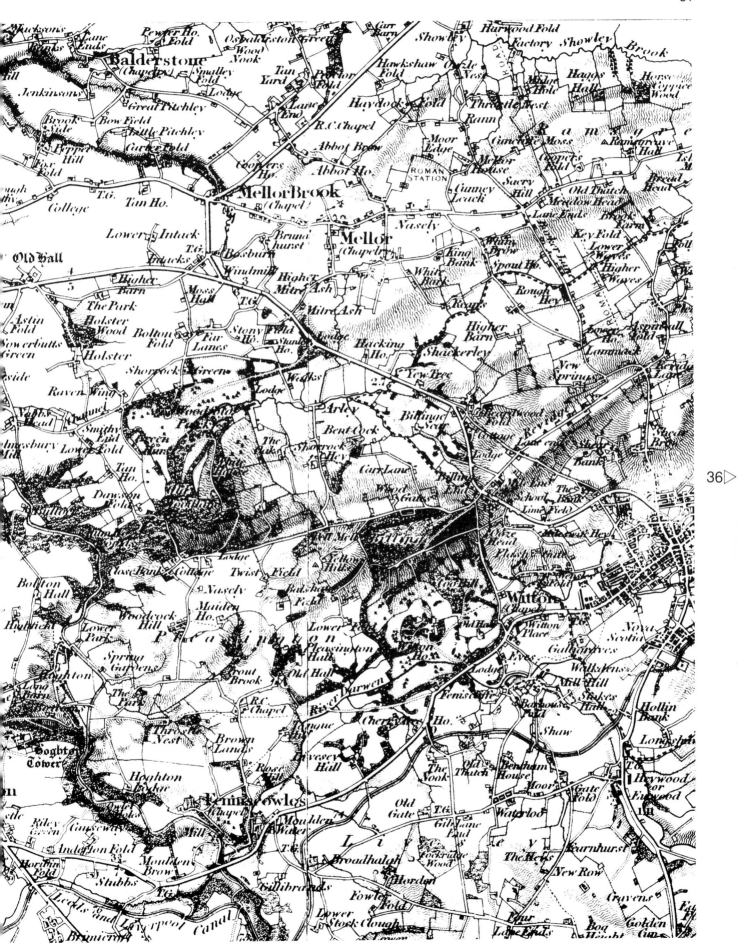

Published 1840 - 1844.

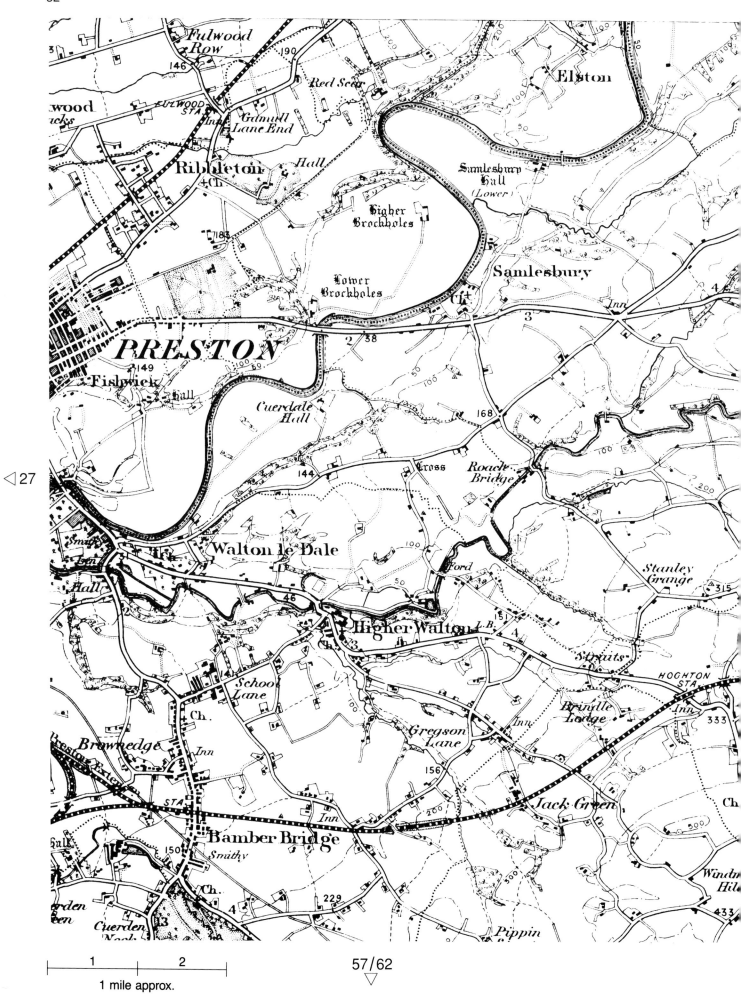

◁27

1 mile approx.

Lane
Ends
236
Osbaldeston Green
323
Showley Fold
400

Osbaldeston
300

Ch.
45
200

Midge
Hall
400

Balderstone
356
6
Inn

Ramsgreave
Hall
500

Inglewood
erscough
Smithy

BEACON
733
700
726
700

Mellor
Brook
Inn
L.B.
641
Inn
Top of Ramsgreave
500
600

Samlesbury Hall
(Higher)
367
Ch.
Mellor

5
Smithy
6
Inn

534
Lammack
690
L.B.

473
Stanley Ho
381
500
400
Inn
Beardwood
Four Lane Ends
600
85
700

Hoolster
Hill
Nab's Head

Billinge
Scarr
700

Samlesbury
Bottoms
200
Woodfold
Park
Shorrock
Hey
Pellmell

38

489
Billinge
Hill
808
700
600

Witton
Park
500
600

lton Hall

Hall
400

Long Barn
Hoghton
Bottoms
300
Old
Hall

Finiscliffe
Ch.
STA.
9
STA.

Tower
556
347
Pleasington
STA.
500
Inn
Hall
Cherry Tree

Old Hall
Ewood

ghton
Ch.
8
Inn
Smithy
Beechwood
400

Feniscowles
Hall
Inn
L I V E S E Y
STA.
Bunker's
Hill
500

ley
een
Horden
600

375
Paper Mill
659

Canal
Brimmicroft

Surveyed 1889 - 93. Revised 1895. Published 1896.

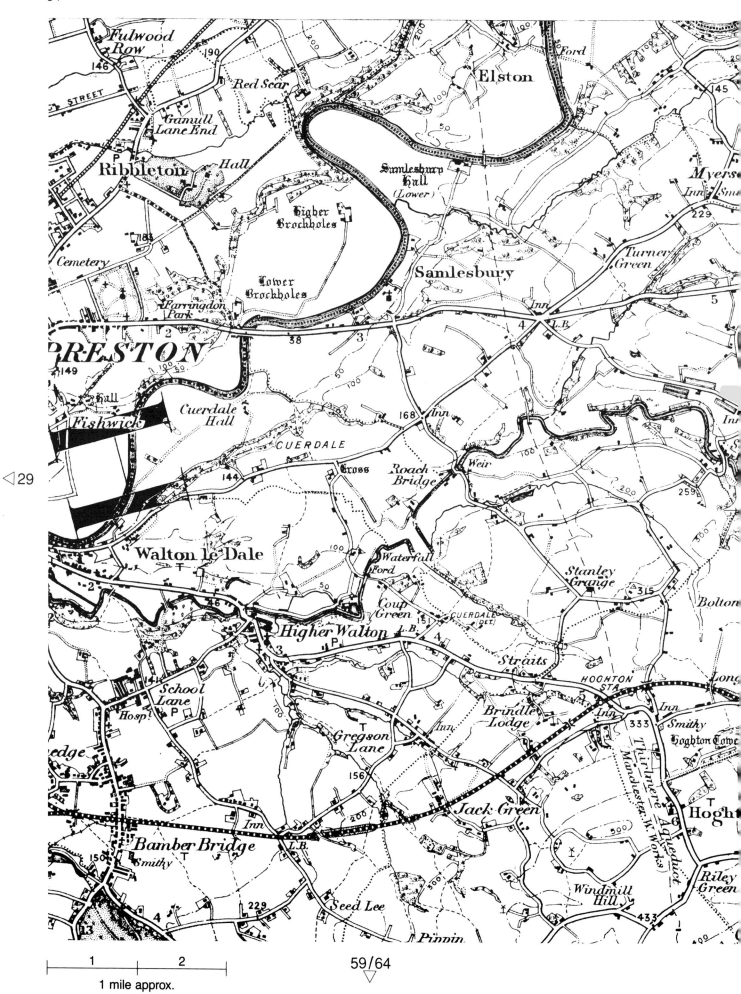

Fulwood Row

146

190

STREET

Red Scar

Gamull Lane End

P

Ribbleton

Hall

183

Cemetery

Higher Brockholes

Farringdon Park

Lower Brockholes

PRESTON

149

Hall

Cuerdale Hall

Fishwick

29

CUERDALE

144

Cross

Roach Bridge

Weir

168

Inn

Walton le Dale

T

Waterfall

Ford

Stanley Grange

315

2

100

46

50

Coup Green

15

CUERDALE DET.

L.B.

Higher Walton

P

3

4

Straits

HOGHTON STA.

School Lane

P

Hosp!

141

Brindle Lodge

333

Smithy

Hoghton Tower

edge

Gregson Lane

156

Inn

Inn

Thirlmere Aqueduct (Manchester W. Works)

Jack Green

6

Hoght

Inn

Bamber Bridge

L.B.

150

Smithy

T

Windmill Hill

433

Riley Green

13

4

229

Seed Lee

J. Pippin

Elston

Ford

145

Samlesbury Hall (Lower)

100

50

Myers

Inn

229

Samlesbury

Turner Green

5

Inn

4

L.B.

38

3

50

100

200

259

200

300

Bolton

1   2

1 mile approx.

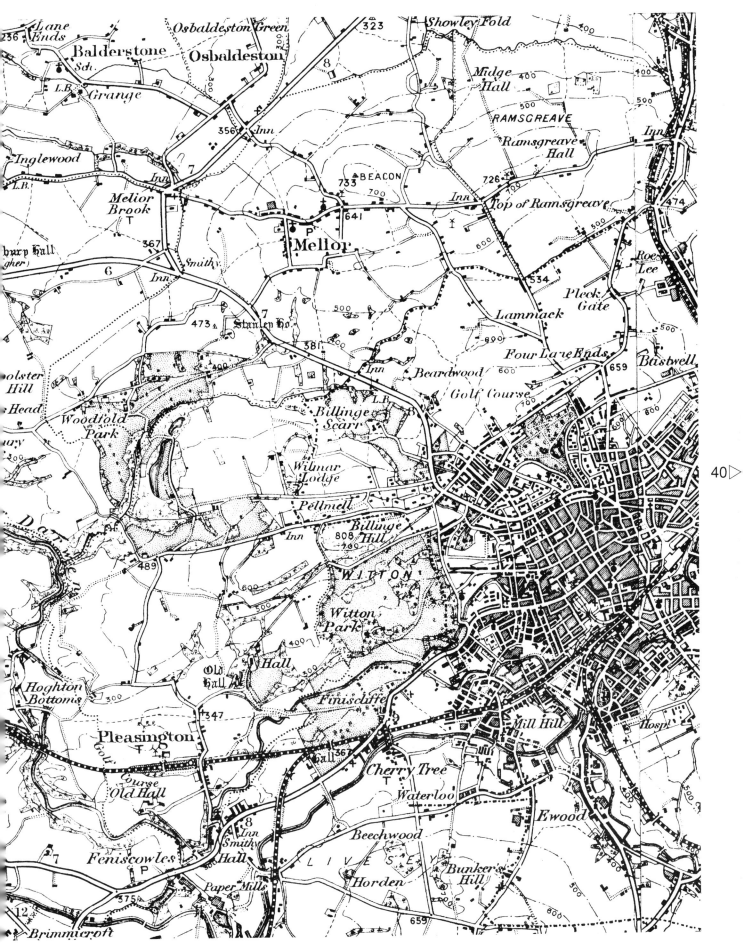

40 ▷

Surveyed 1842 - 44 / 1888 - 93. Revised 1912. Published 1913.

1 mile approx.

42▷

Published 1840 - 1844.

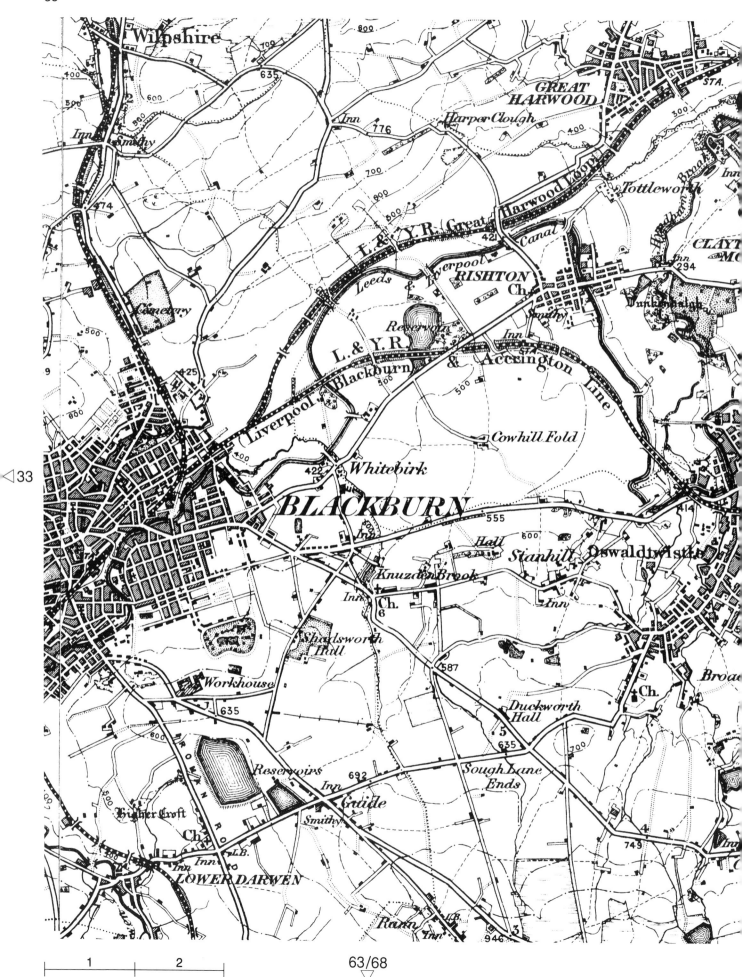

1 mile approx.

Hyndburn Bridge
240
Clayton Hall
300
433
Shuttleworth Hall
389
Inn Hapton
425
STA

Higher Firs
474
400
500
500
Huncoat
Inn
618
572
Hall
Inn
Lane Ends
Old Barn
Birch Range
800
600
700
800
1000

Lane Side
Cemetery
Reservoirs
Hillock Vale
535
600

Church
Ch
Ch
Ch
ACCRINGTON
High Riley
Moleside Moor
Great Hameldon
1343
1164
Hameldon
1305
Reservoir
1250
1250
1102

Hey
Collins
664
600
Clifton
L. & Y. R.
700
800
The Laund
800
946
Reservoirs
1250
Love Clough
1215

Inn
600
Bedlam
700
Accrington & Colne
Inn
Baxenden
HENHEADS
Goodshaw Fold
HIGHE
Ilkthorn
874
900
2
Rising Bridge
Inn
Goodshaw
3
Brook
883
960
1000
2
Acre
Crabden Side

44 ▷

Surveyed 1889 - 92. Revised 1892. Published 1896.

◁35

1   2

1 mile approx.

65/70
▽

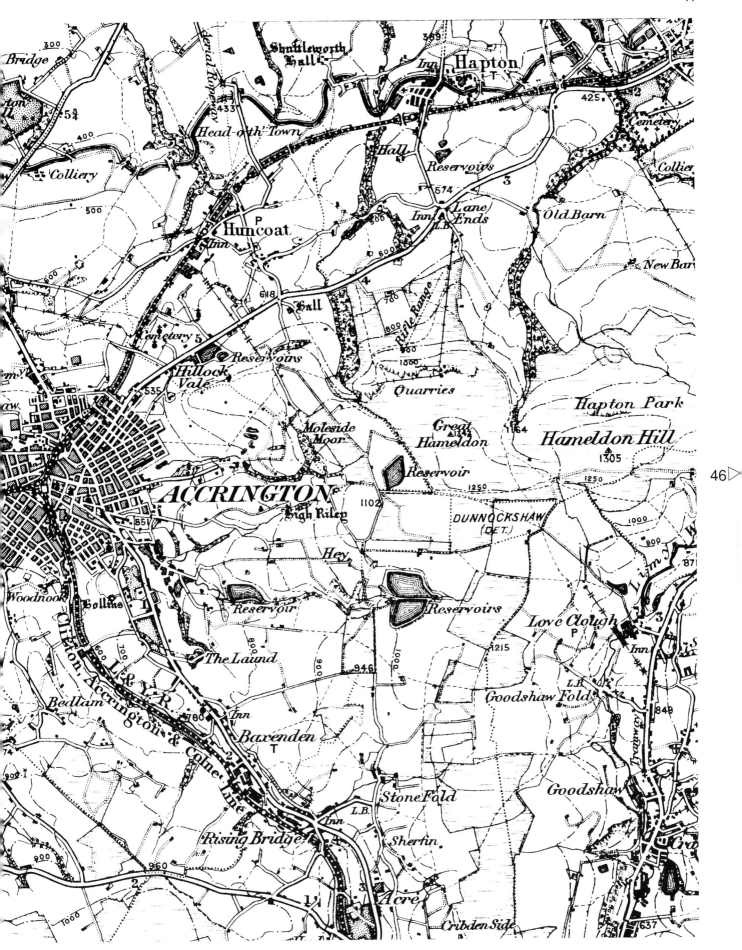

Surveyed 1888 - 93. Revised 1912. Published 1913.

◁37

1   2

1 mile approx.

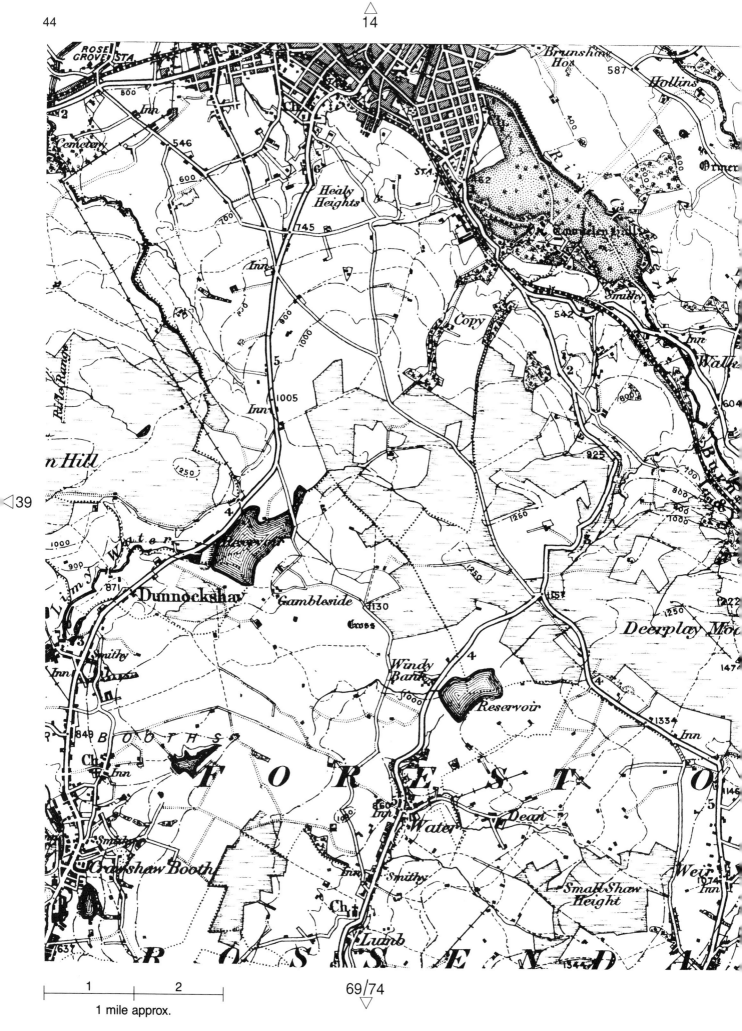

1 mile approx.

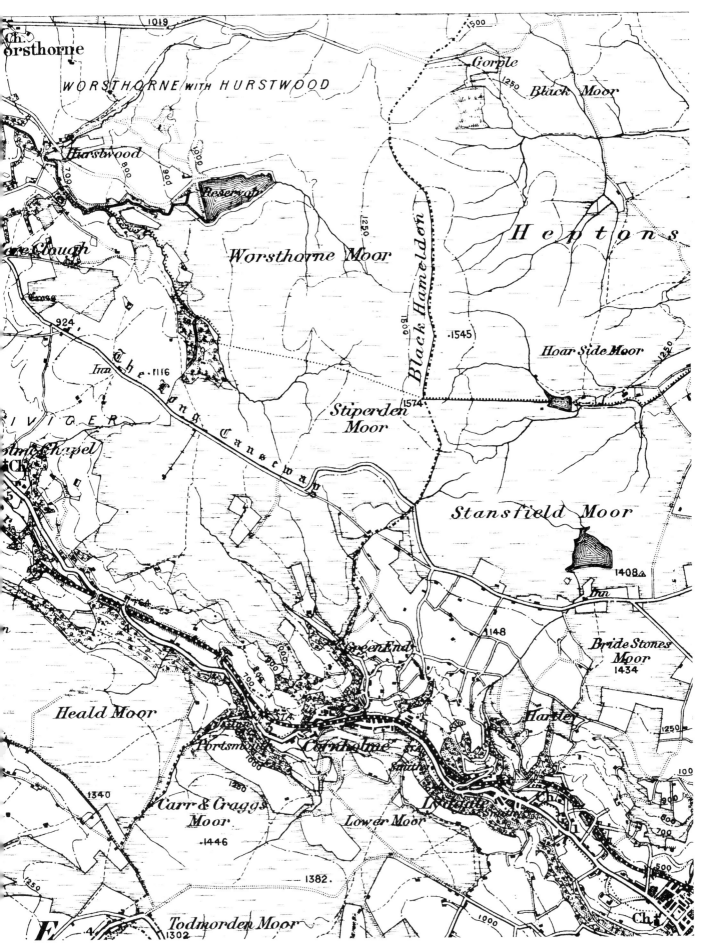

Surveyed 1889 - 92. Revised 1892. Published 1896.

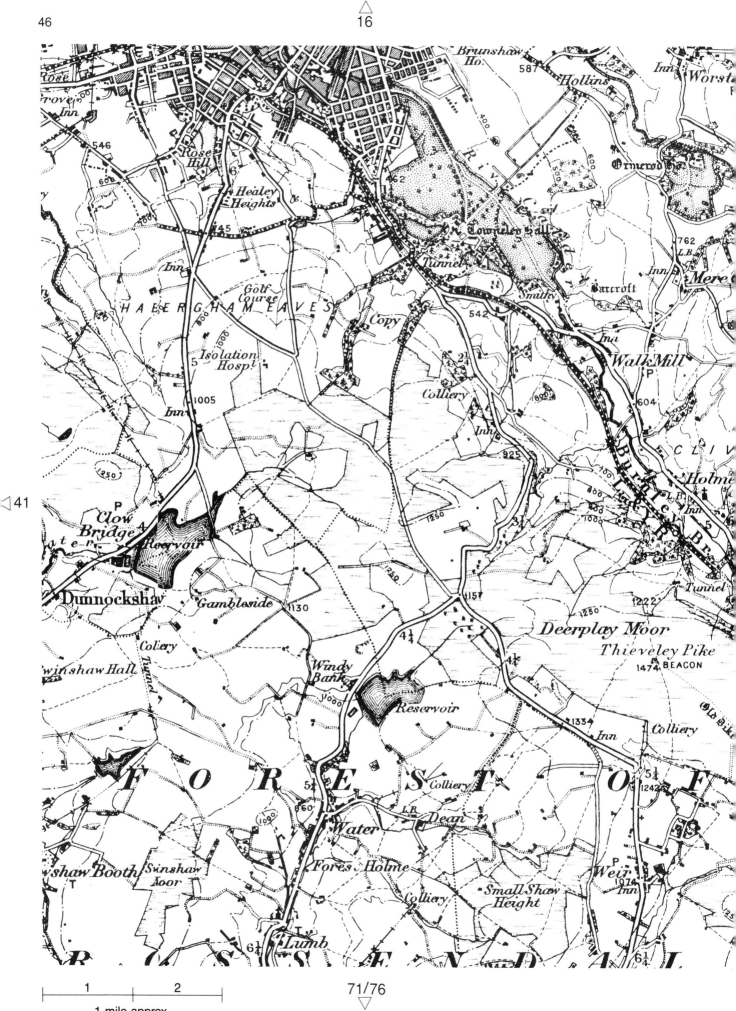

1   2

1 mile approx.

Surveyed 1888 - 93. Revised 1912. Published 1913.

△

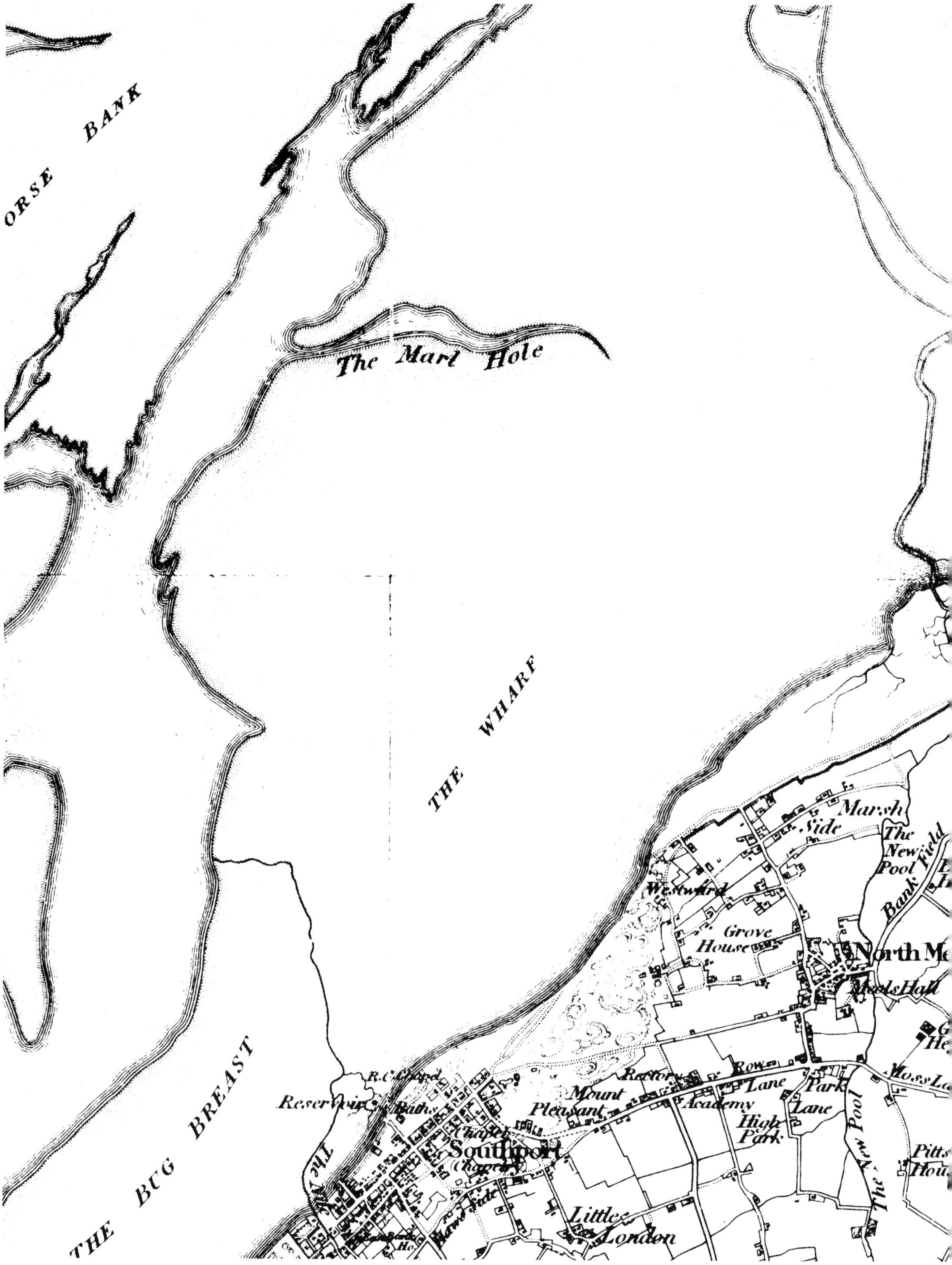

ORSE BANK

THE BUG BREAST

The Marl Hole

THE WHARF

Marsh Side

The Newfield

Bank Field

Westward

Grove House

North Me

Meols Hall

G
He

Rectory Row

Lane

Park Lane

R.C.Chapel

Mount Pleasant

Academy

Moss La

Reservoir

Baths

High Park

The New Pool

Pitts Hou

Chapel

Southport
(Chapel)

New Fold

Little London

Ho

1		2

1 mile approx.

▽

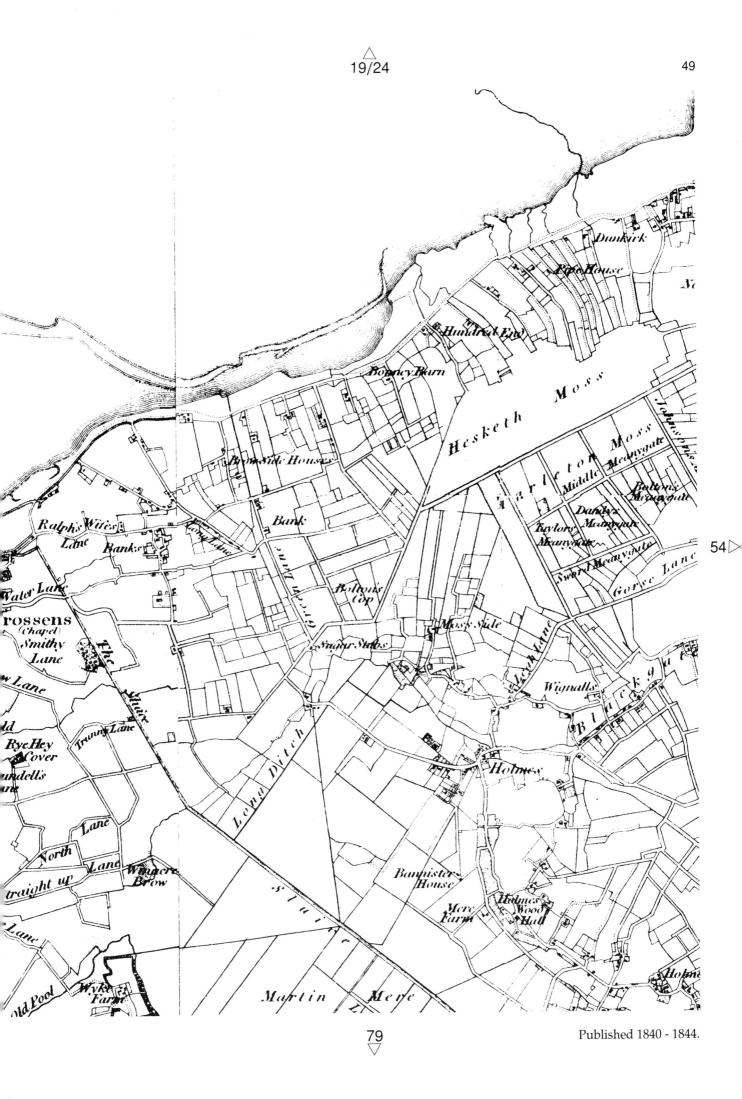

Published 1840 - 1844.

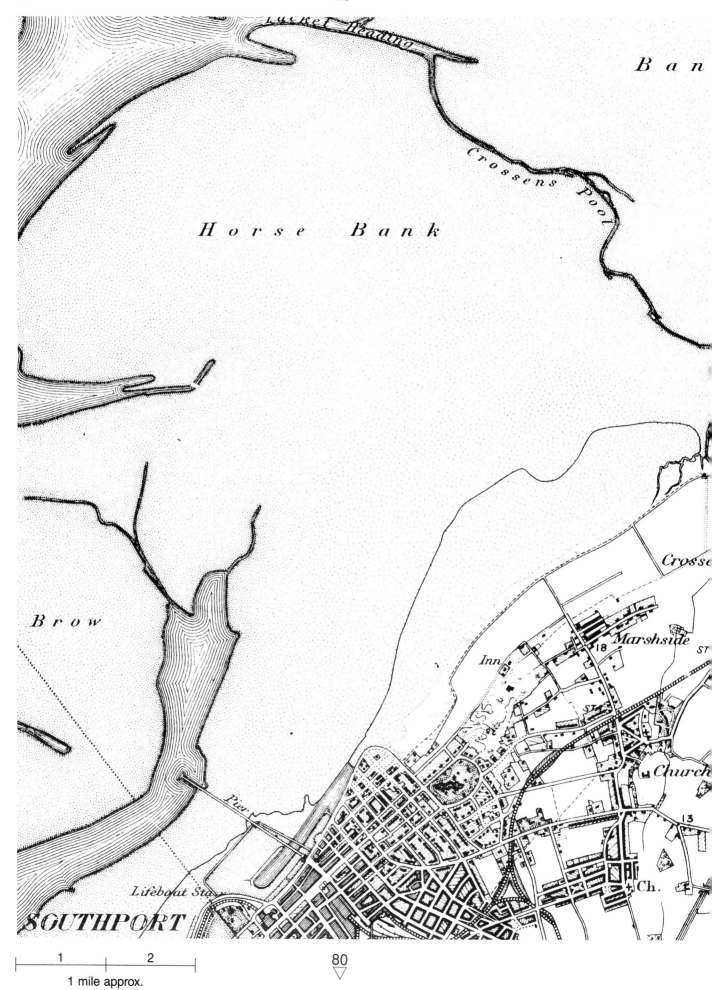

Bank

Rucket Heading

Crossens Pool

Horse Bank

Brow

Crosse

Marshside

Inn

18

Church

Pier

13

Lifeboat Sta.

Ch.

SOUTHPORT

80

1   2

1 mile approx.

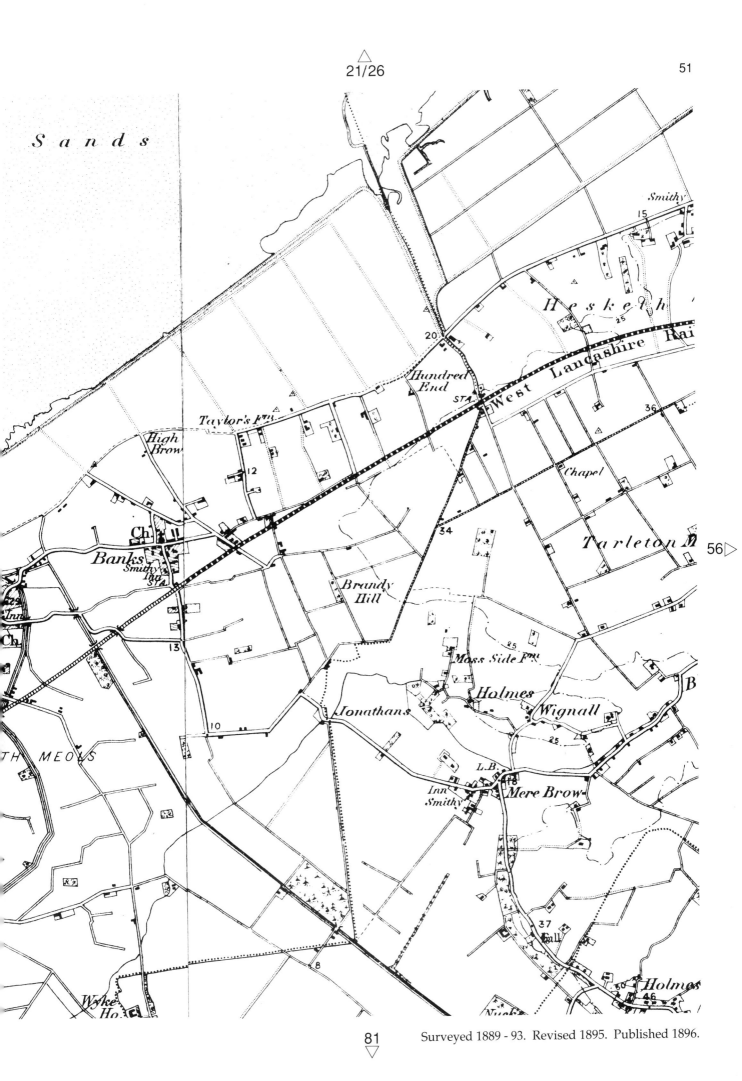

S a n d s

Smithy

15

H e s k e t h

25

20

Hundred End

STA.

West Lancashire Rai

36

Taylor's F^m

High Brow

12

Chapel

34

Tarleton M

△ 56 ▷

Ch.

Banks

Smithy's Inn STA.

Brandy Hill

25

Moss Side F^m

Holmes Wignall

B

13

Jonathans

25

10

MEOLS

L.B.

18

Inn Smithy

Mere Brow

37

Mill

Holmes

46

8

Wyke Ho.

Surveyed 1889 - 93. Revised 1895. Published 1896.

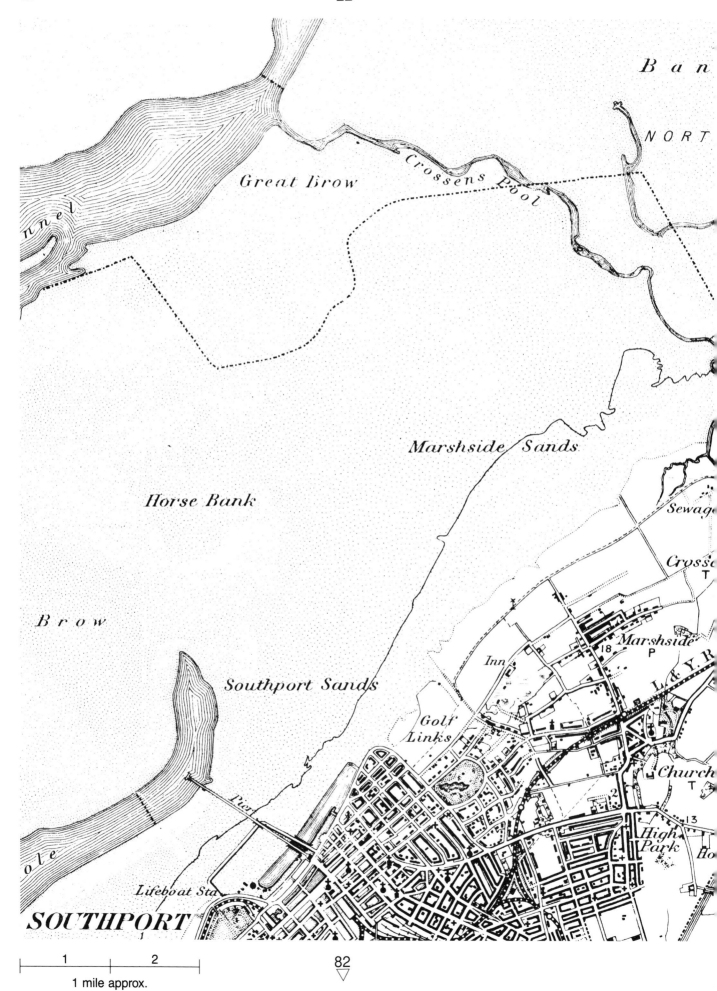

B a n

NORT

Great Brow

Crossens Pool

Marshside Sands

Sewage

Horse Bank

Cross

T

B r o w

Marshside

18 P

Inn

L & Y R.

Southport Sands

*Golf
Links*

Church

T

2

13

Pier

*High
Park*

ole

Ho

Lifeboat Sta.

SOUTHPORT

1

1	2

1 mile approx.

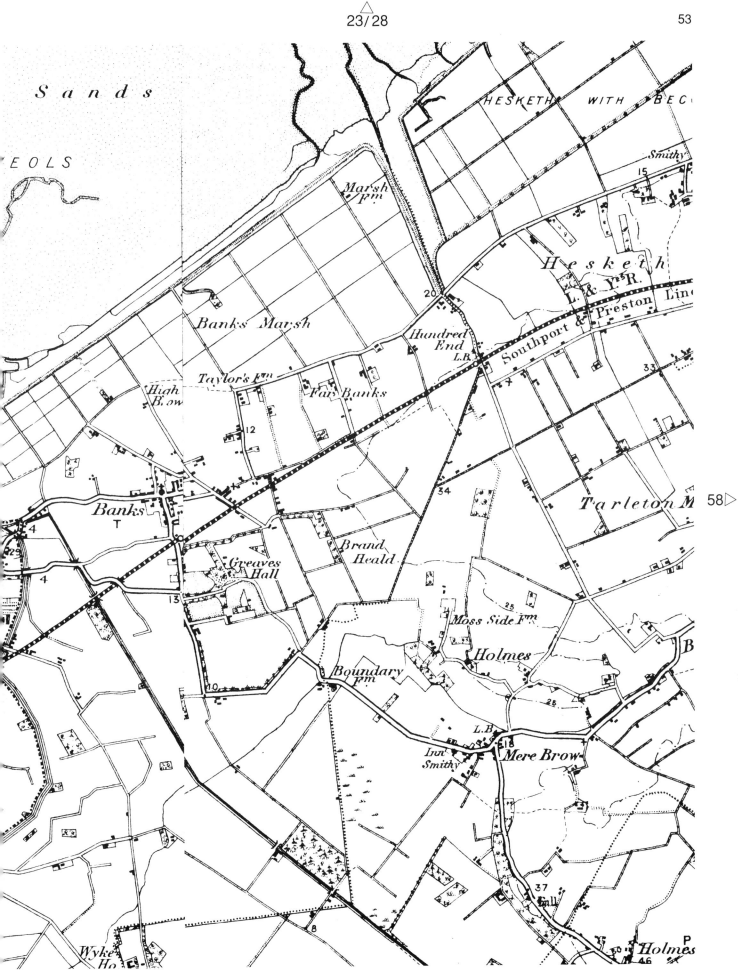

Surveyed 1888 - 93. Revised 1912. Published 1913.

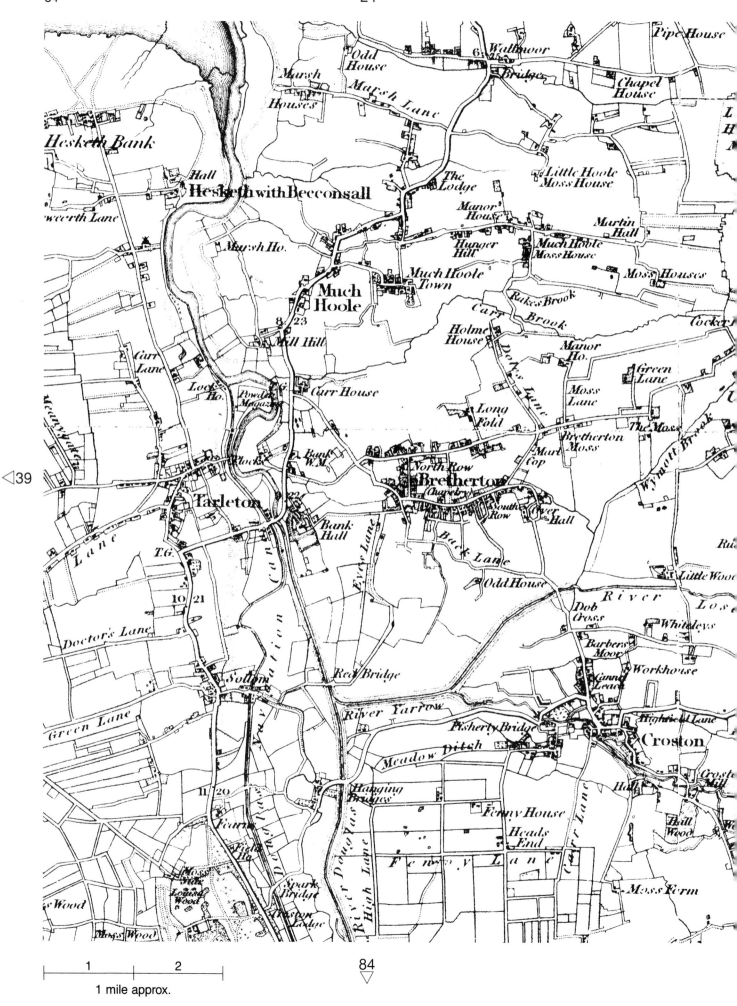

1   2

1 mile approx.

Published 1840 - 1844.

△
26

Moor Side

Hall

Odd Ho.

6
Inn

Walmer Bridge

HOOLE STA.

LITTLE HOOLE

41

Marsh Fm.

Inn

Hesketh Bank

59

△
Pleas View

Becconsall Hall *Ch.*

Much Hoole

Inn *Smithy*
7

47 △
54

Goose Green 50

Much Hoole Moss Houses

HESKETH BANK STA. *Inn*

lway

25

Inn

Ch.
35

△

Mill Hill
8

18

37

Lock

Carr Ho.

△51

Moss

59

Smithy

25

Windmill

Bretherton *Inn*
Ch.

25

Tarleton *Ch.*

Smithy
9

Smithy

25

ULNE

Inn

36

Ch.

Bank Hall

ackgate Lane

10

25

Barber's Mo

STA.

Sollom

Smithy *Inn* *Croston*
Ch.

Red Br.
12

18

Hall
32

11

25

20

Grea Hanging Br.

16

Leeds & Liver

Wood

River Dou

86
▽

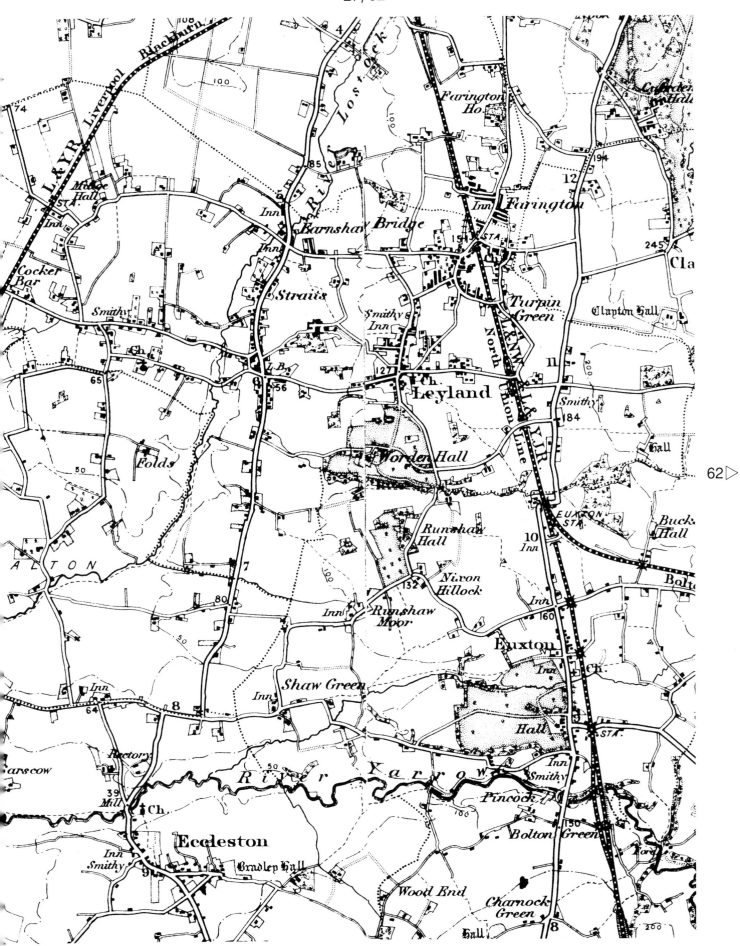

62▷

Surveyed 1847 - 49. Revised 1895. Published 1896.

Moor Side

CONSALL

Odd Ho.

Inn

Walmer
Bridge

LITTLE HOOLE

HOOLE STA.

Inn

Marsh F^m

Hesketh Bank

P

Becconsall

Much Hoole

P

Plea...
View

Smithy

47

154

Inn

Goose Green

Much Hoole
Moss Houses

T

Inn

Much Hoole
Town

Mill Hill

8

33

59

18

37

Carr Ho.

53

HALT

Lock

25

HALT

Windmill

Bretherton

P

25

Tarleton

T

9

Bank Hall

Cross

ULNE...

36

...ackgate Lane

Barber's Mo...

10

Croston
T

Sollom

Red Br.

L.B.

42

8

Hall

25

Great Hanging Br.

32

Leeds & Liv...

20

RIVER DOU...

16

...wood

| 1 | 2 |

1 mile approx.

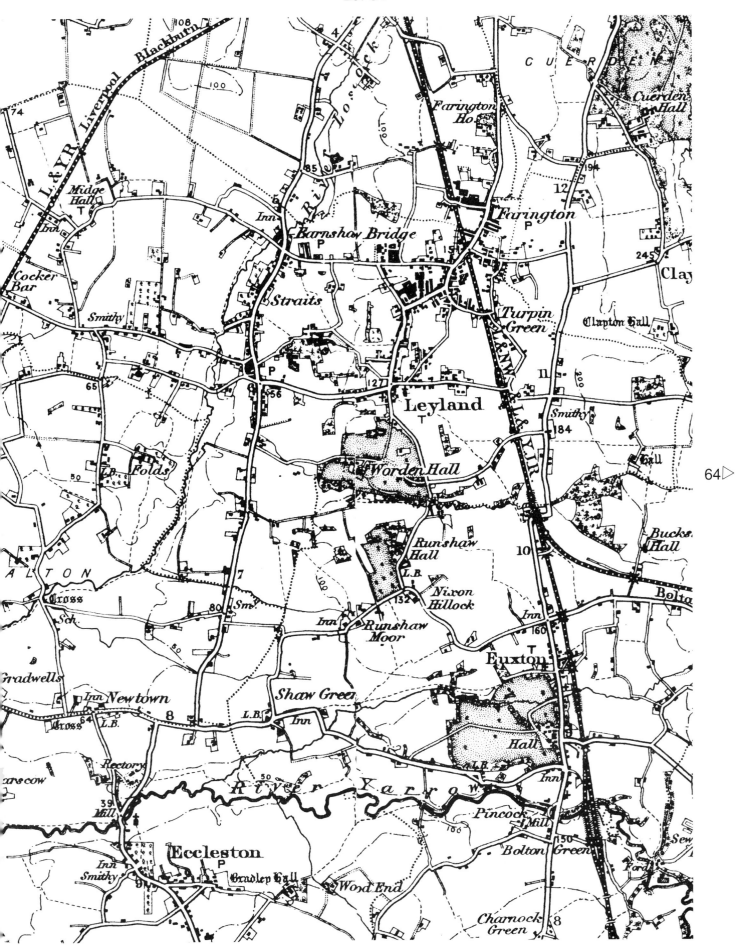

Surveyed 1888 - 93. Revised 1912. Published 1913.

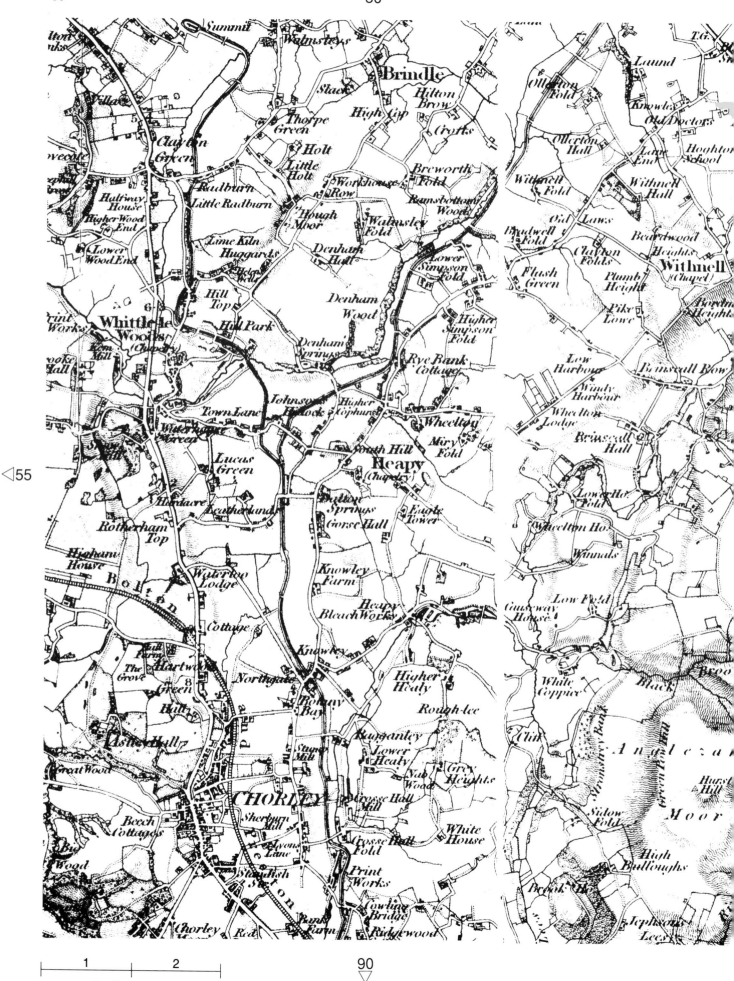

Summit

Walmsleys

Brindle

Stack

Hilton
Brow

High Gip

Crofts

Laund

Knowles

Old Doctors

Ollerton
Fold

Thorpe
Green

Holt

Little
Holt

Breworth
Fold

Workhouse
Row

Ramsbottom
Wood

Ollerton
Hall

Lane
End

Hoghton
School

Withnell
Fold

Withnell
Hall

Beardwood

Withnell
(Chapel)

Clayton
Green

Radburn

Little Radburn

Hough
Moor

Walmsley
Fold

Lower
Simpson
Fold

Old Laws

Bradwell
Fold

Clayton
Folds

Beardwood
Heights

Halfway
House

Higher Wood
End

Lime Kiln
Huggards

Denham
Hall

Flash
Green

Plumb
Height

Lower
Wood End

Helga
Well

Denham
Wood

Higher
Simpson
Fold

Pike
Lowe

Borden
Heights

Hill
Top

Hill Park

Denham
Springs

Rye Bank
Cottage

Low
Harbour

Brinscall Brow

Whittle
Woods
(Chapel)

Windy
Harbour

Print
Works

Ken
Mill

Johnson

Higher
Copthurst

Wheelton

Mary
Fold

Wheelton
Lodge

Brinscall
Hall

Brooke
Hall

Town Lane

Hillock

Watermans
Mercer

South Hill

Heapy
(Chapelry)

Lucas
Green

Sculpt
Mill

Hindaire

Leatherlands

Sutton
Springs

Gorse Hall

Eagle
Tower

Lower Ho.
Fold

Wheelton Ho.

Winnals

55

Rotherham
Top

Knowley
Farm

Low Field

Causeway
House

Higham
House

Bolton

Waterloo
Lodge

Heapy
Bleach Works

Higher
Healy

White
Coppice

Black

Broo

Cottage

Knowley

Clin

Anglezar

The
Grove

Hartwood
Green

Northgate

Bottony
Bay

Rough-lee

Hurst
Hill

Hall

Pincock

Banganley

Sidow
Fold

Moor

Astley Hall

Sturgeon
Mill

Lower
Healy

Vale
Wood

Grey
Heights

White
Coppice

Great Wood

CHORLEY

Crosse Hall
Mill

High
Bullloughs

Beech
Cottages

Sherburn
Mill

Lyons
Lane

Crosse Hall
Fold

White
House

Brook Hill

Jephsons
Lees

Big
Wood

Standish
Sutton

Print
Works

Chorley Rd

Bank
Farm

Cowling
Bridge

Ridgewood

T.G.

1   2

1 mile approx.

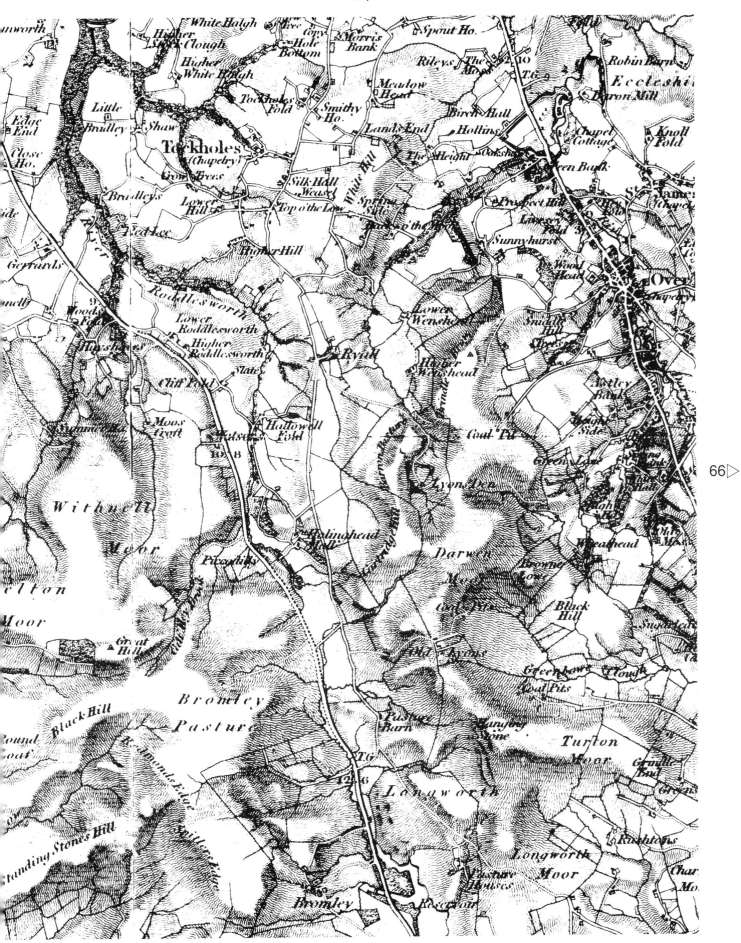

Published 1840 - 1844.

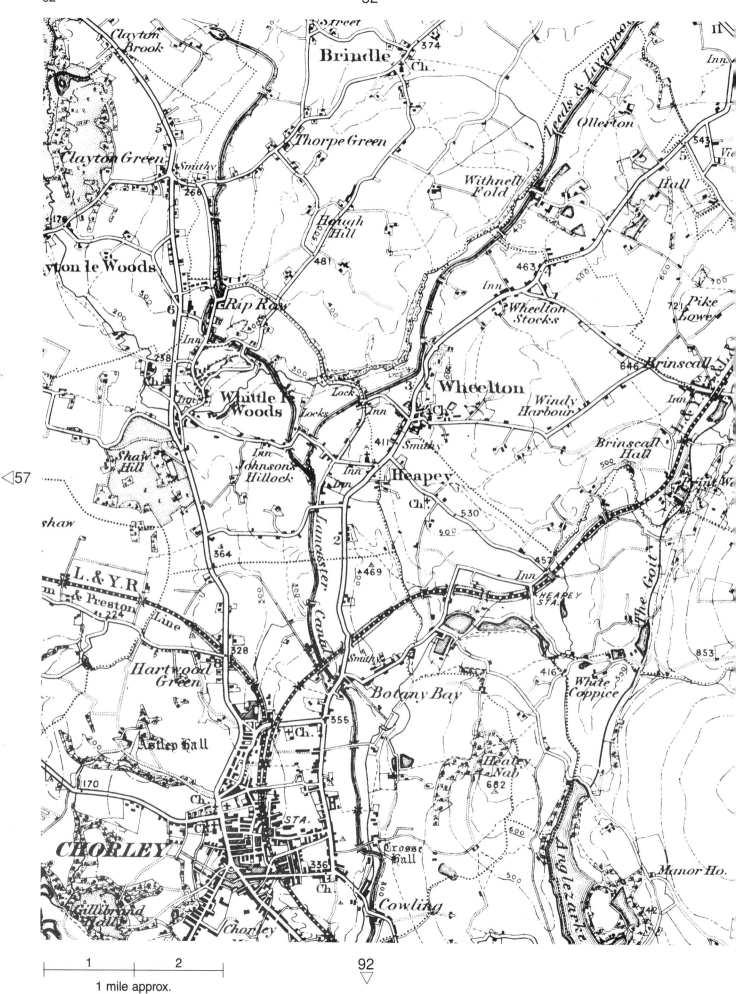

Street

Brindle

374

Ch.

Clayton
Brook

Inn

Leeds & Liverpool

Ollerton

543

Inn

Thorpe Green

Clayton Green

Smithy

266

Withnell
Fold

Hall

176

Hough
Hill

400

500

600

700

481

463

Inn

600

ton le Woods

500

500

Wheelton
Stocks

721

Pike
Lowe

6

Rip Row

258

400

300

646

Brinscall

Inn

Ch.

Whittle
Woods

Lock

3

Wheelton

Windy
Harbour

Brinscall
Hall

△57

Locks

4 Ch.

500

Johnsons
Hillock

Inn

411

Smithy

Shaw
Hill

Inn

Inn

Heapey

Ch.

Brink We

shaw

Lancaster Canal

2

530

500

500

364

469

457

Inn

The Goit

L. & Y. R.

Preston

224

Line

HEAPEY
STA.

328

Smithy

416

853

Hartwood
Green

White
Coppice

500

Botany Bay

170

355

Astley Hall

Heapey
Nab

682

Ch.

Anglezark

Ch.

600

CHORLEY

STA.

Ch.

336

Crosse
Hall

500

librand
all

Ch.

Cowling

Manor Ho.

742

Chorley

1

2

1 mile approx.

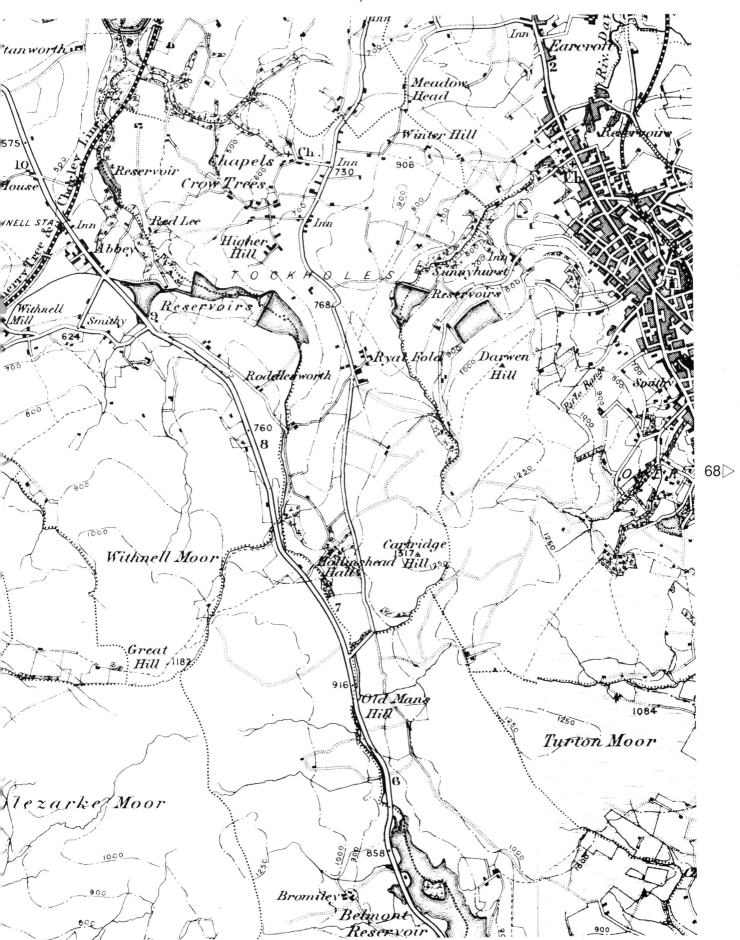

Surveyed 1889 - 92. Revised 1892. Published 1896.

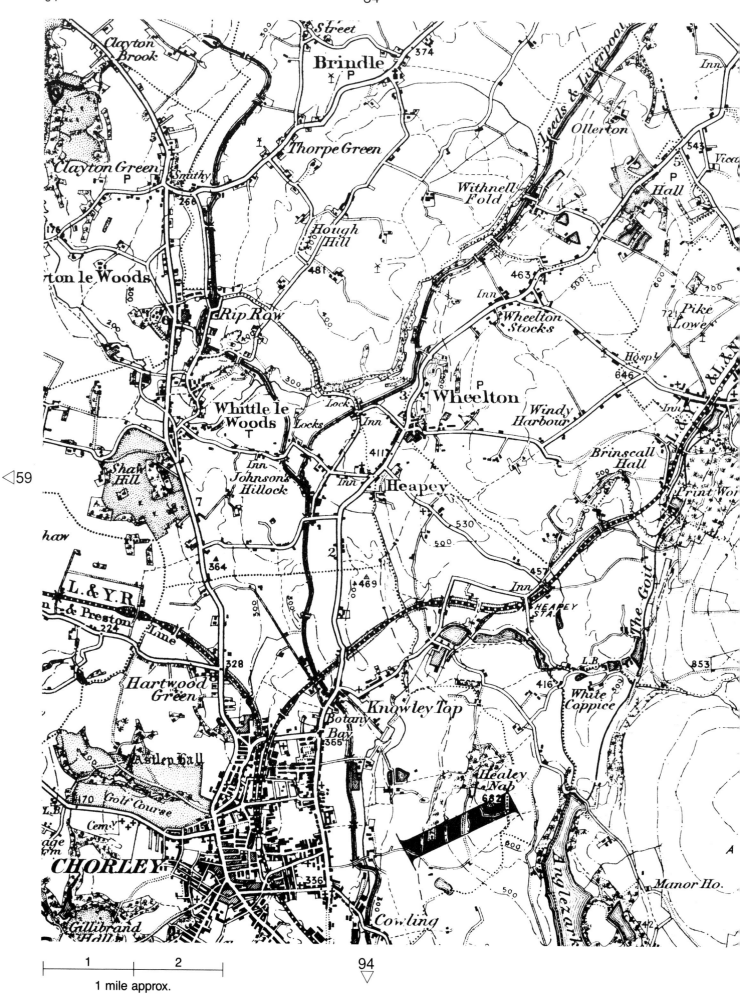

Clayton
Brook

Street

BRINDLE
P
374

Leeds & Liverpool

Ollerton

Inn

Clayton Green
P

Thorpe Green

Withnell
Fold

543

Vica

Hall
P

ton le Woods

Hough
Hill

481

Wheelton
Stocks

463

Pike
Lowe

72

Rip Row

Hosp!

646

◁59

Lock

Wheelton
P

Windy
Harbour

Inn

& L. & N

Whittle le
Woods
T

Locks

3

Inn

Brinscall
Hall

Shaw
Hill

Inn
Johnsons
Hillock

411

Inn

Heapey

Print Wor

haw

364

2

530

500

469

457

Inn

The Golt

L. & Y.R

& Preston Line

328

300

853

416

L.B.

White
Coppice

Hartwood
Green

Knowley Top

Botany
Bay

365

HEAPEY
STA

Astley Hall

Healey
Nab
682

170

Golf Course

L.B.

Cem?

600

CHORLEY

336

500

Manor Ho.

A

Gillibrand
Hall

Cowling

Anglezark

1   2

1 mile approx.

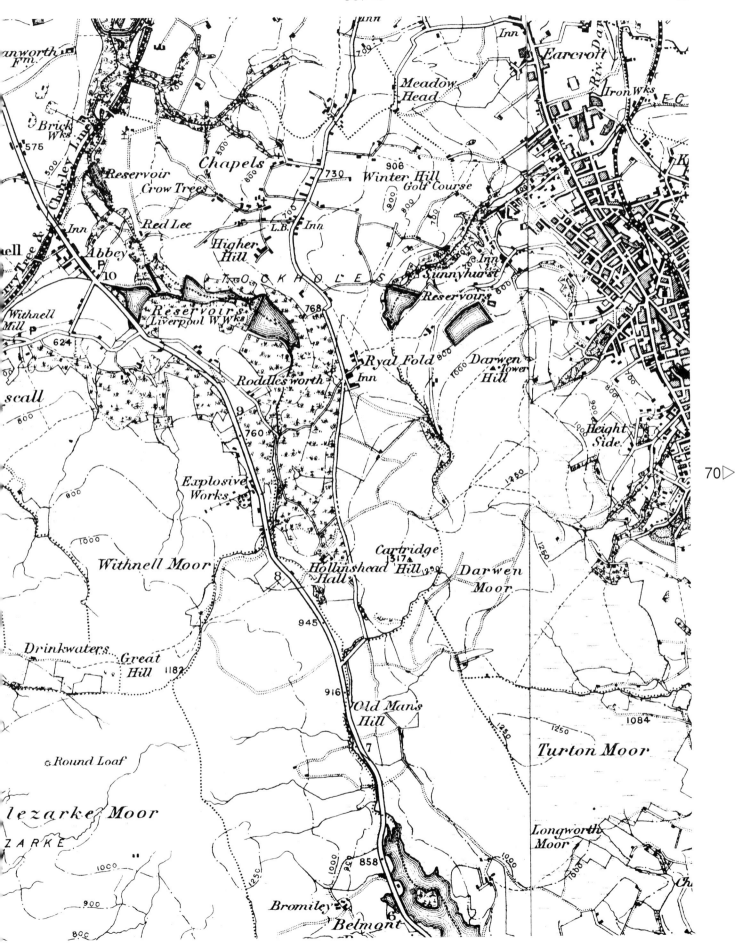

Surveyed 1888 - 93. Revised 1912. Published 1913.

1   2

1 mile approx.

Published 1840 - 1844.

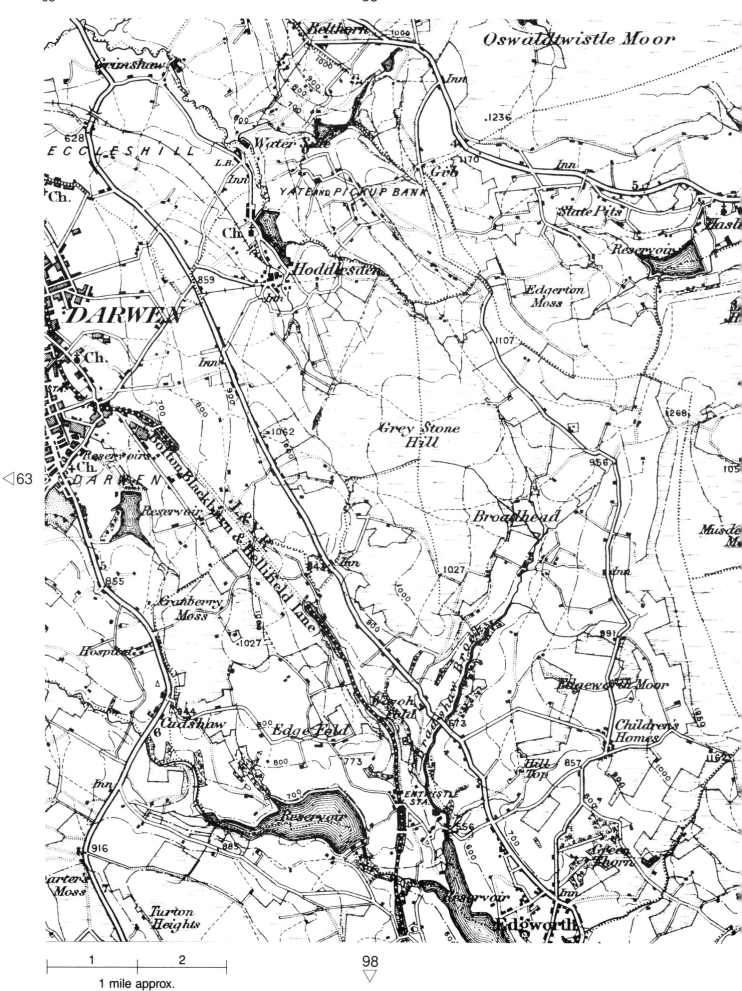

Belthorn

Oswaldtwistle Moor

1000

Grimshaw

900

800

700

628

ECCLESHILL

L.B.

Water Side

Inn

YATE AND PICKUP BANK

Gvo

Inn

.1236

1170

Inn

Slate Pits

Ch.

Reservoir

Hasl

Ch.

Hoddlesden

Edgerton Moss

859

Inn

DARWEN

Ch.

Inn

1107

Grey Stone Hill

1268

956

⊲63

Reservoirs

Ch.

DARWEN

Reservoir

800

900

700

1062

1000

105

Broadhead

Bolton Blackburn & Hellifield Line

Reservoir

1027

5

855

Inn

800

1027

Cranberry Moss

Inn

Edgeworth Moor

Inn

991

Hospital

944

Cadshaw

800

Edge Fold

Bough Fold

773

857

1103

Hill Top

Children's Homes

1000

916

885

Reservoir

700

Inn

ENTWISTLE STA.

1256

Green Thorn

600

arters Moss

7

Turton Heights

800

Reservoir

Idgworth

Inn

1   2

1 mile approx.

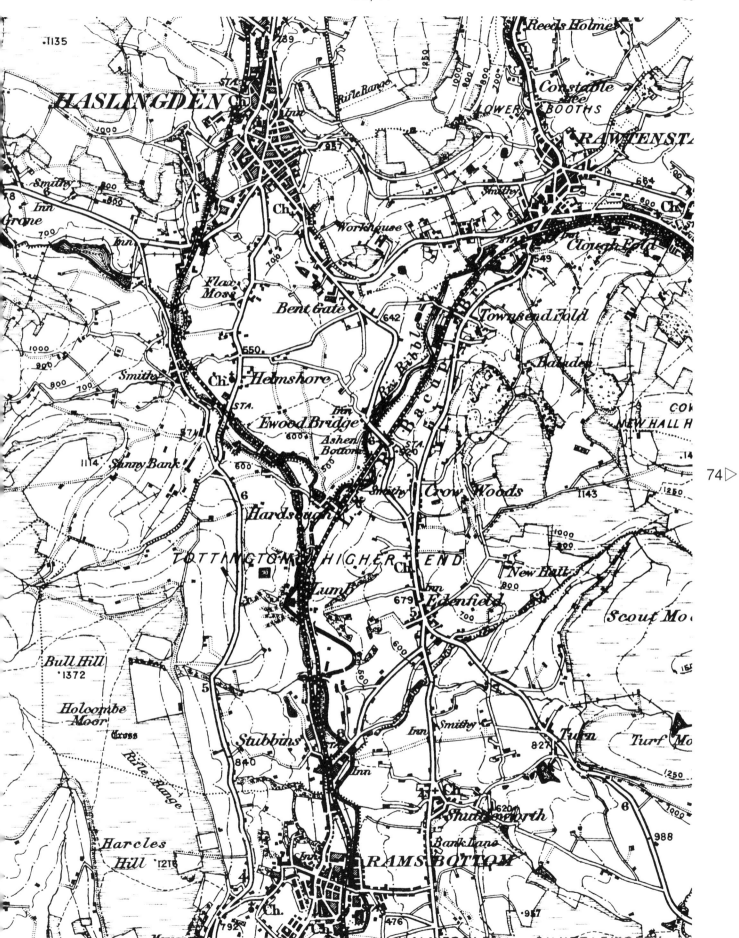

Surveyed 1847 - 49. Revised 1895. Published 1896.

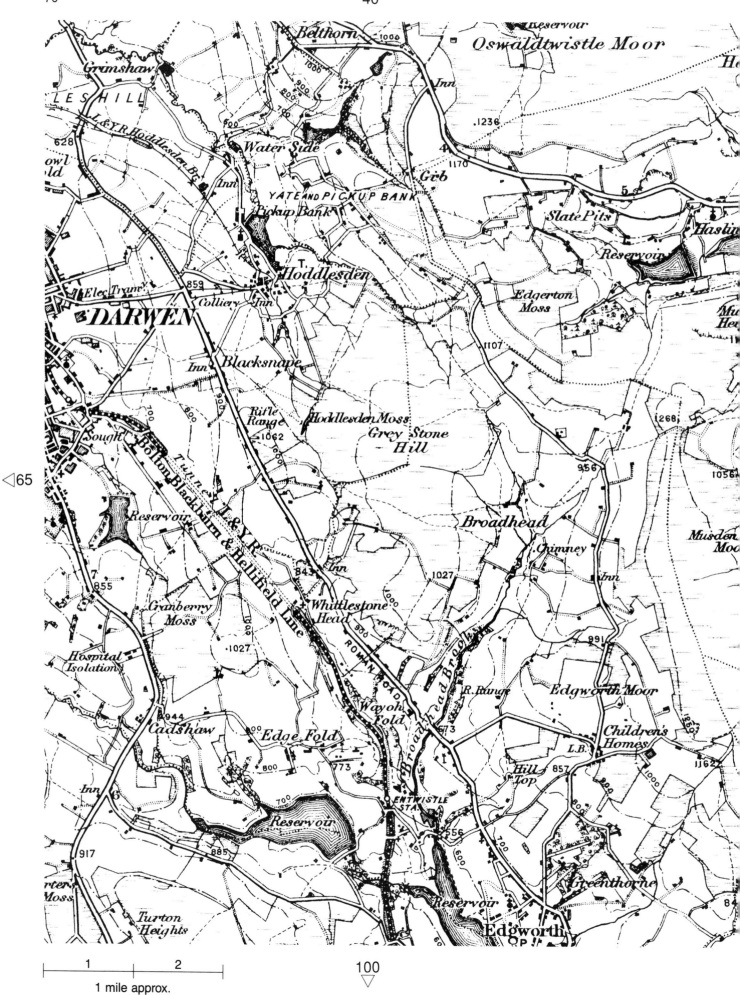

Reservoir

Oswaldtwistle Moor

Belthorn

1000

Grimshaw

900

800

LES HILL

Inn

L&Y.R. Hoddlesden Br.

900

.1238

628

1170

owl
ld

Water Side

Gcb

5

Inn

Slate Pits

YATE AND PICKUP BANK

Reservoir

Hasli

Pickup Bank

Hoddlesden

T

Edgerton
Moss

Mu
Hea

Elec Tram

859

DARWEN

Colliery Inn

1107

Blacksnape

Inn

Rifle
Range

Hoddlesden Moss

.1062

*Grey Stone
Hill*

(268)

Sough

800

956

1056

700

900

◁65

Reservoir

Broadhead

Musden
Moo

1027

Gimney

7
855

Inn

843 Inn

1000

*Cranberry
Moss*

*Whittlestone
Head*

900

991

.1027

ROMAN ROAD

Hospital
Isolation

R. Range

Edgworth Moor

1260

944

*Wayoh
Fold*

673

*Children's
Homes*

Cadshaw

Edge Fold

L.B.

I

Hill
Top   857

1000

1162

800

773

900

700

800

ENTWISTLE
STA.

700

Inn

600

Reservoir

556

700

917

885

Greenthorne

8

Reservoir

*Turton
Heights*

rter
Moss

600

Edgworth

1   2

1 mile approx.

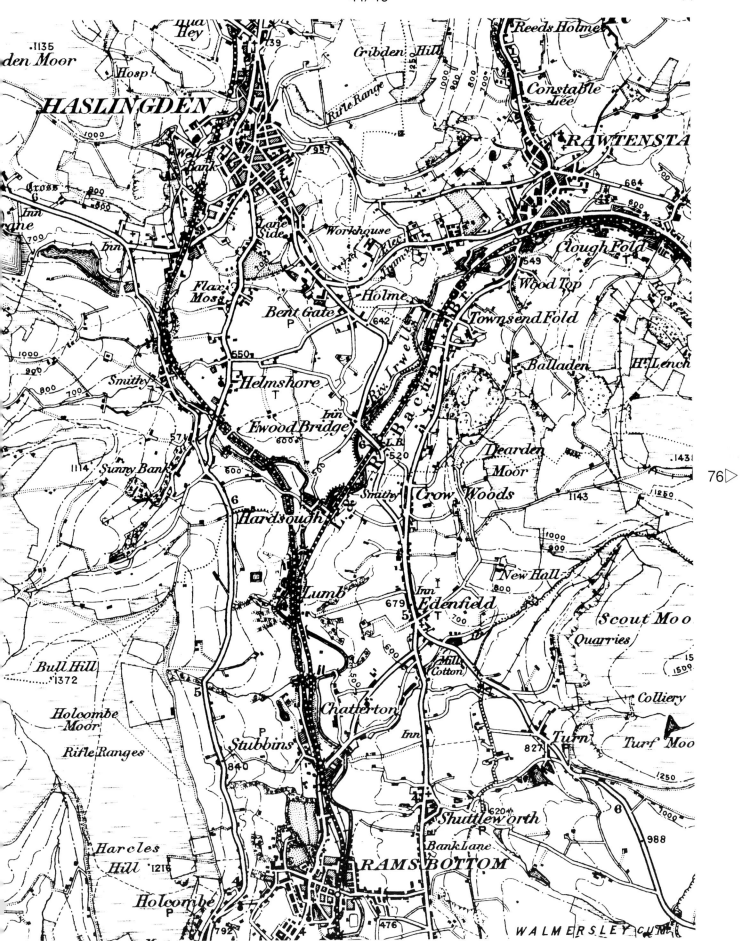

Surveyed 1888 - 93. Revised 1912. Published 1913.

1   2

1 mile approx.

Published 1840 - 1844.

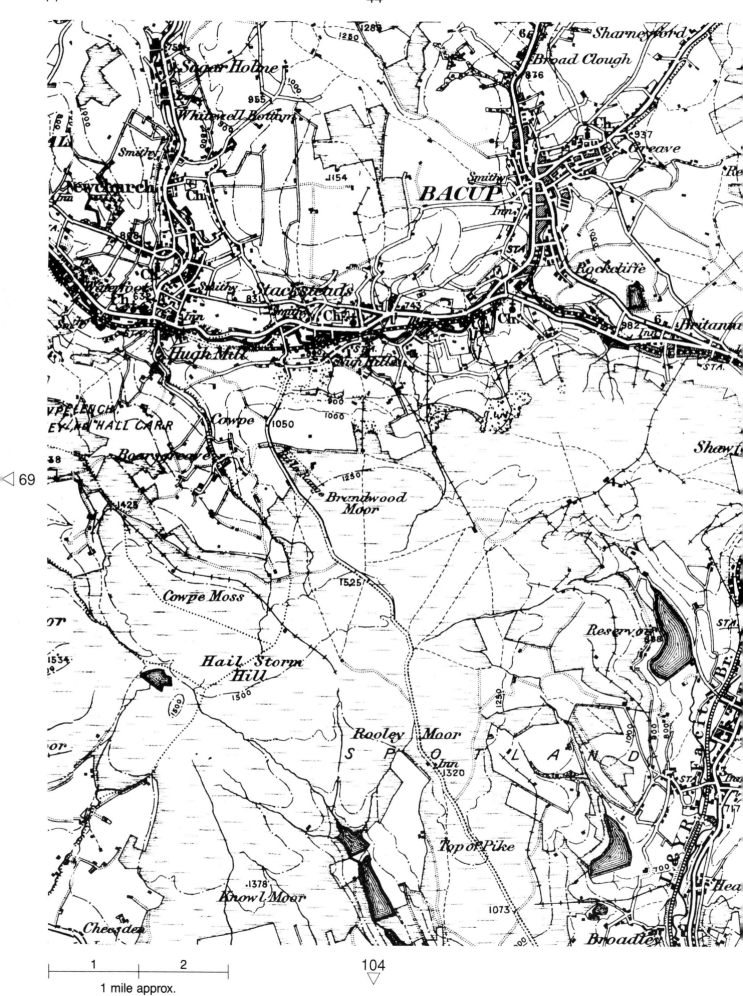

Sharneyford

Broad Clough

876

Ch. 937

Greave

Sugar Holme

955

Whitewell Bottom

1000

Smithy

1250

1280

65

BACUP

Smithy

Inn.

Newchurch

Inn.

Ch.

1154

STA.

Rockcliffe

Ch.

858

Waterfoot

Ch.

Stacksteads

831

743

Smithy

Ch.

Smithy

Smithy

982

6. Britannia

Inn.

Hugh Mill

STA.

STA.

VP.LENCH

EY & HALL CARR

Cowpe

1050

1000

900

1438

Boarsgreave

Shaw

Brandwood

Moor

1250

Reservoir

Cowpe Moss

1525

1534

Hail Storm

Hill

1500

1500

1250

Reservoir

Rooley Moor

S P

O

T

L

A N D

Inn.

1320

800

Top of Pike

700

1378

Knowl Moor

1073

Broadley

Cheesden

Hea

1   2

1 mile approx.

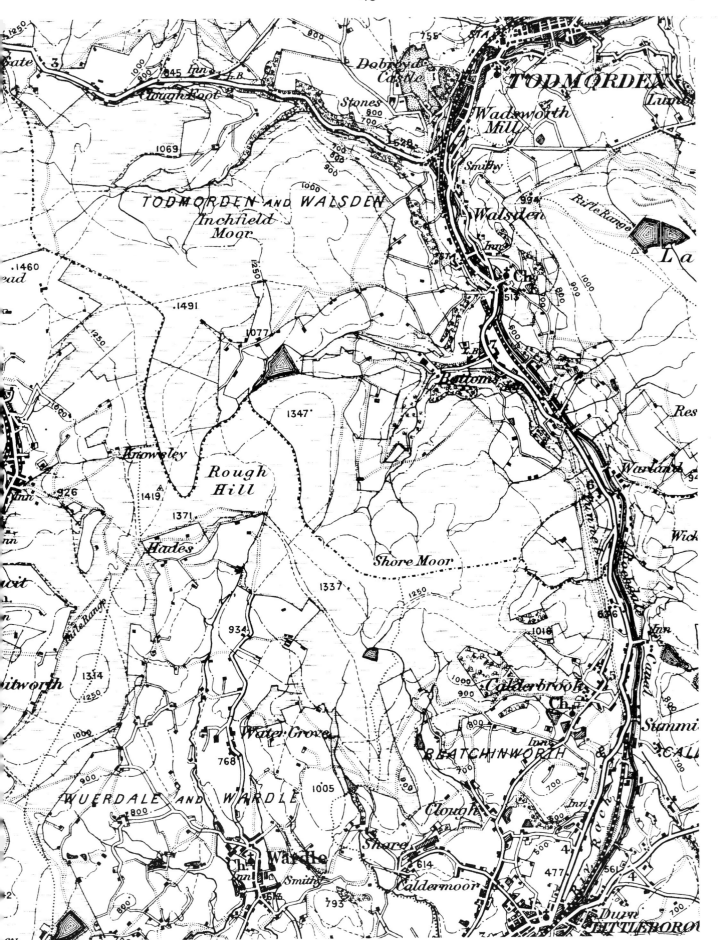

Surveyed 1847 - 49. Revised 1895. Published 1896.

1

2

1 mile approx.

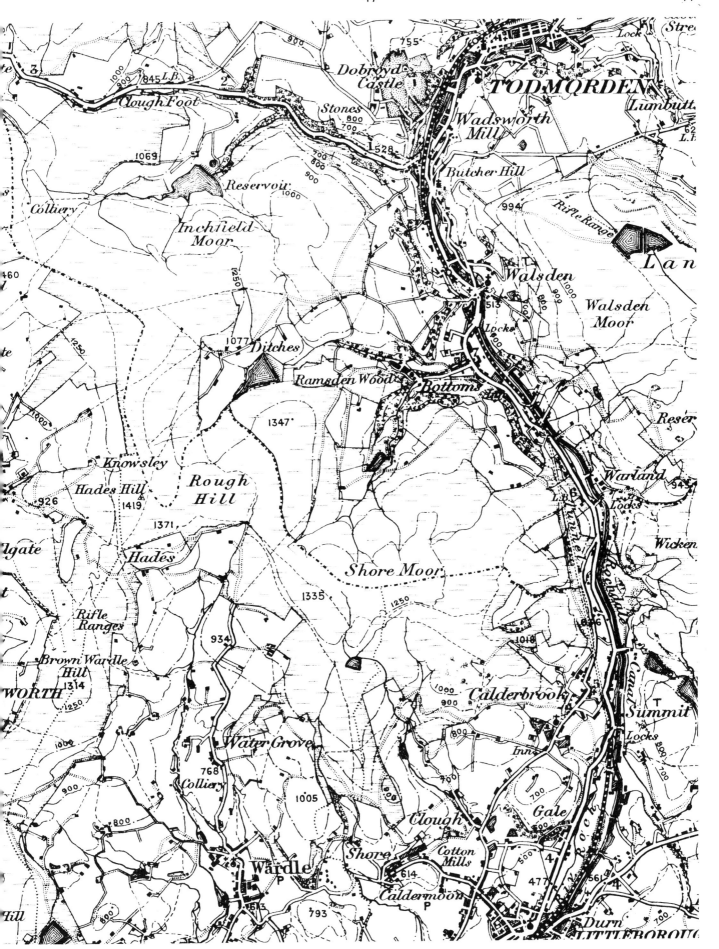

Surveyed 1888 - 93. Revised 1912. Published 1913.

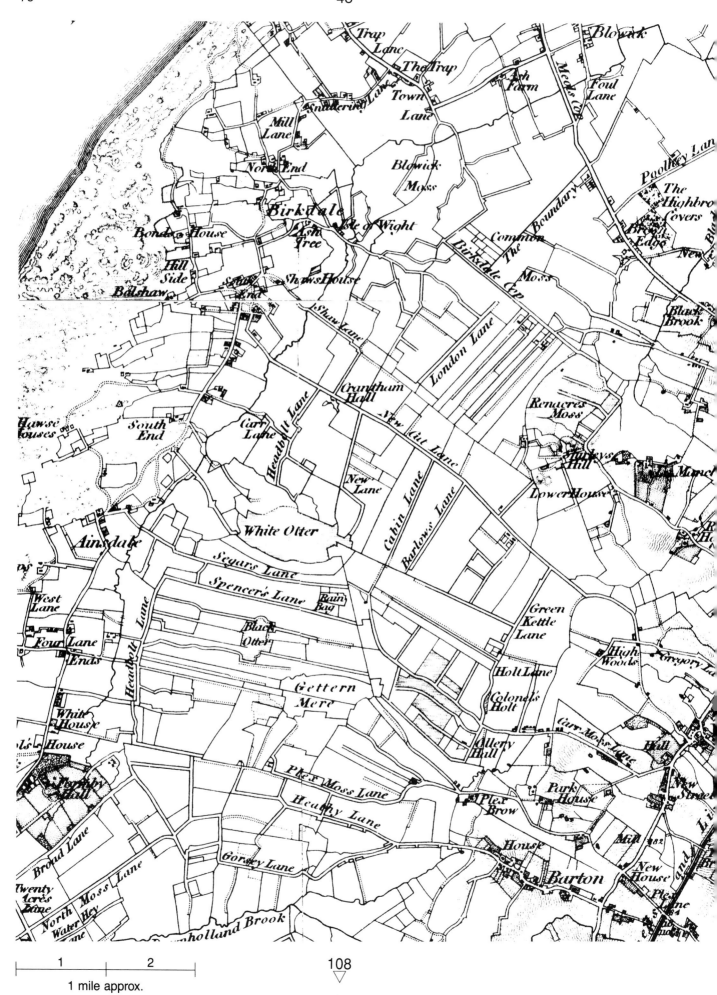

Blowick

Trap Lane

The Trap

Meols Cop

Ash Farm

Foul Lane

Snittering Lane

Town Lane

Poolhey Lane

Mill Lane

Blowick Moss

The Highbro Covers

North End

Boundary

Brock Edge

Birkdale

The Common

New

Isle of Wight

Bonkers House

Ash Tree

Birkdale Cop

Moss

Black Brook

Hill Side

Shaws House

Belshaw

South End

Shaws Lane

London Lane

Renacres Moss

Hawse Houses

South End

Carr Lane

Grantham Hall

New Cut Lane

Shirleys Hill

Marsh

Headbolt Lane

Lower House

New Lane

Cabin Lane

Barlows Lane

White Otter

Ainsdale

Segars Lane

Spencer's Lane

Rain Bag

Green Kettle Lane

West Lane

High Woods

Gregory La

Four Lane Ends

Black Otter

Holt Lane

Headbolt Lane

Gettern Mere

Colonel's Holt

White House

Carr Moss Lane

Hall

's House

Ollery Hall

Formby Hall

Plex Moss Lane

Park House

New Stree

Broad Lane

Heathy Lane

Plex Brow

House

Mill

New House

Barton

Plex Lane

Twenty Acres Lane

Gorsey Lane

North Moss Lane

Water Hey Lane

holland Brook

1   2

1 mile approx.

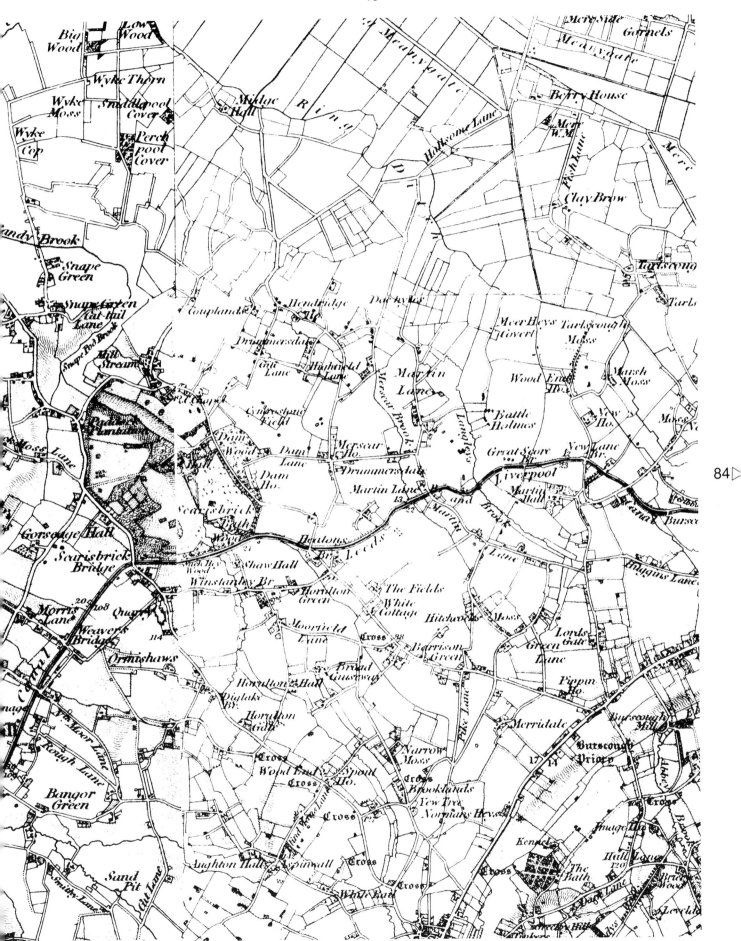

Published 1840 - 1844.

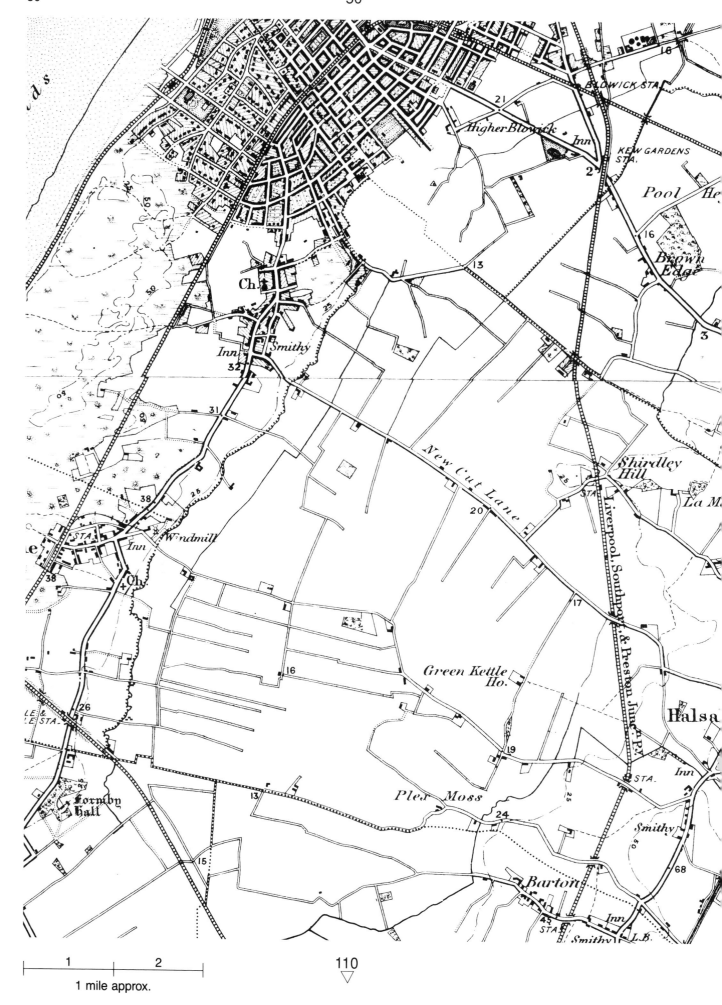

50

Higher Blowick Inn

21

BLOWICK STA.

KEW GARDENS STA.

2

Pool He

16

Brown Edge

13

3

Ch.

Inn Smithy

32

31

New Cut Lane

Shirdley Hill

25

La M

38

28

20

STA.

Liverpool, Southport, & Preston Junct. Ry.

17

Windmill

Inn

STA.

Ch.

38

16

Green Kettle Ho.

26

LE & LE STA.

Halsa

19

STA.

Inn

25

Formby Hall

13

Plex Moss

24

Smithy

15

68

Barton

45 STA.

Inn

Smithy L.B.

1   2

1 mile approx.

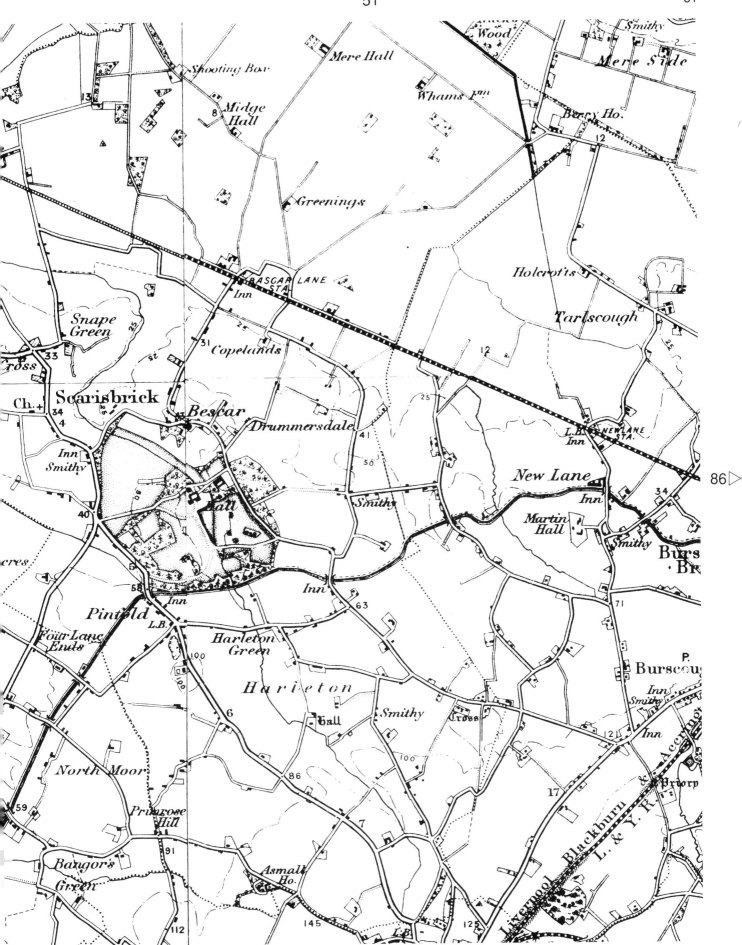

Surveyed 1889 - 93. Revised 1892 / 5. Published 1896.

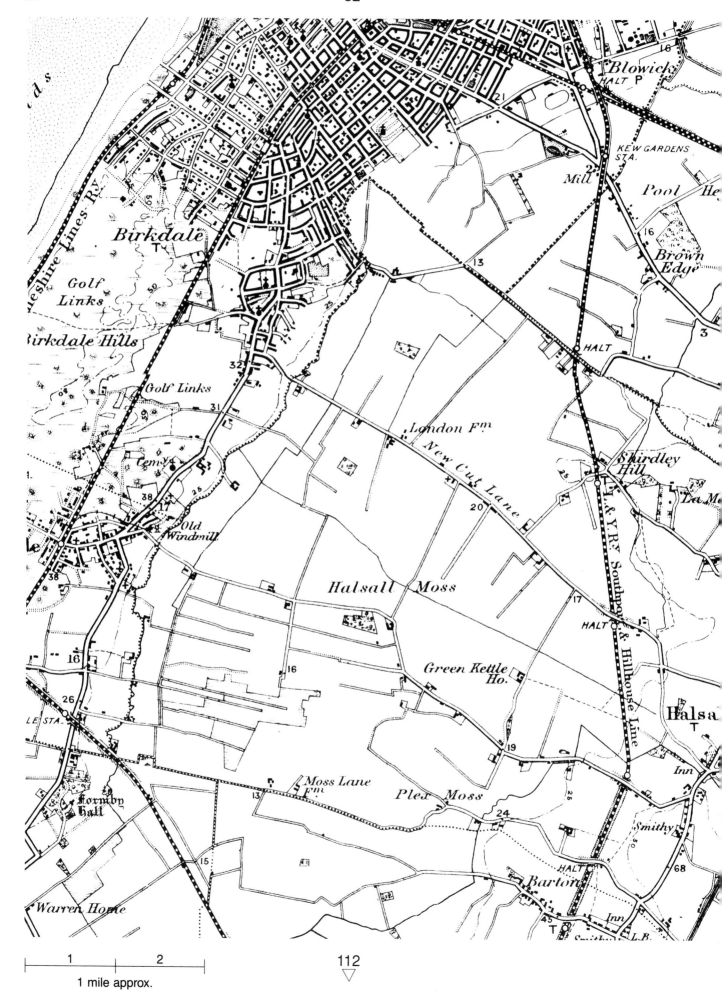

Blowick

HALT P

KEW GARDENS STA.

Pool He

Mill

Brown Edge

Birkdale

T

Golf Links

Birkdale Hills

13

HALT

Golf Links

London Fm

Shirdley Hill

La M

New Cut Lane

Cem. Yd

Old Windmill

20

Halsall Moss

17

HALT

16

Green Kettle Ho.

Halsa

T

26

LE STA.

19

Inn

Moss Lane Fm

13

Plex Moss

24

Formby Hall

Smithy

15

HALT

Barton

Inn

T

Warren Home

L. & Y. Ry. Southport & Hillhouse Line

1   2

1 mile approx.

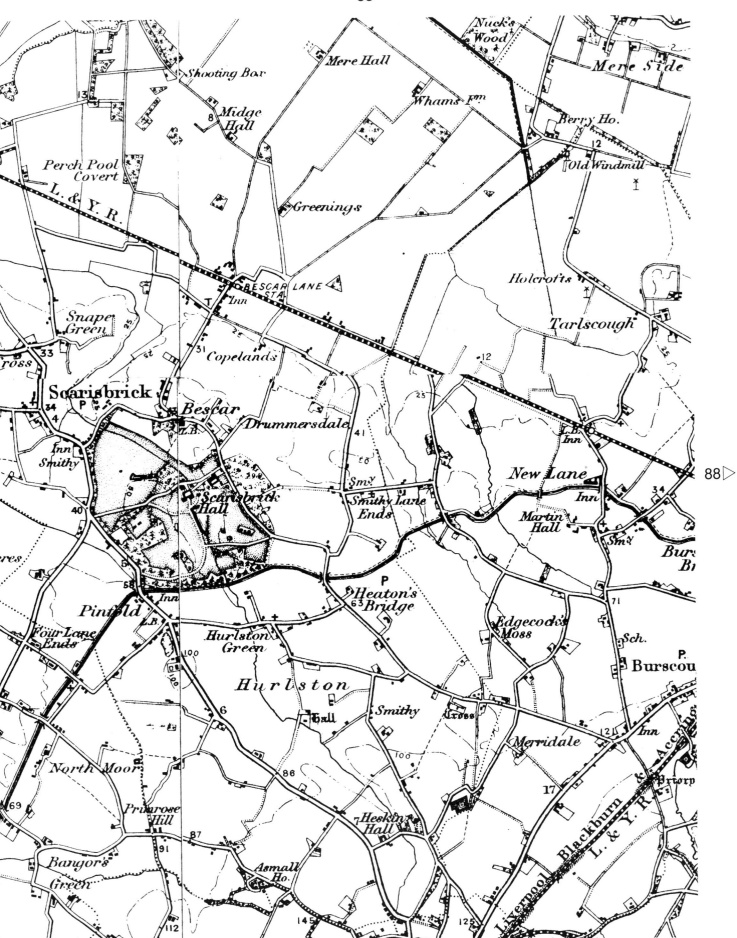

Nuck's Wood

Mere Side

Mere Hall

Whams Fm

Berry Ho.

12

Old Windmill

Shooting Box

Midge Hall

8

Perch Pool Covert

Greenings

L. & Y. R.

Holcrofts

Tarlscough

BESCAR LANE STA.

Inn

Snape Green

25

Copelands

31

25

12

ross

33

34

Scarisbrick

Bescar

L.B.

Drummersdale

41

25

L.B.

Inn

New Lane

Inn

88

4

Inn Smithy

Smy

Smithy Lane Ends

Martin Hall

Smy

40

Scarisbrick Hall

Burs B

50

P

Heaton's Bridge

63

71

Edgecock's Moss

Sch.

Pinfold

Inn

L.B.

Four Lane Ends

Hurlston Green

Hurlston

Burscou

P.

Merridale

121

Inn

North Moor

Hall

Smithy

Cross

100

100

100

86

17

69

Primrose Hill

87

Heskin Hall

Priorp

91

Bangor's Green

Asmall Ho.

Liverpool Blackburn & Accrin

L. & Y. R.

112

145

125

Surveyed 1844 - 47 / 1888 - 93. Revised 1910 - 12. Published 1912 - 13.

Croston Moss

Spring Lane

Red Cap Lane

Hall

12

Lodge

Ice Ho.

Old Hall

Old Douglas

Moss Side

Moss Ho.

Back House

Mere Sands Wood

Nursery

Mawdesley Hall

Mere End

Rufford

Douglas Bridge

Hurst Green

Tooter Ho.

Hall

Raised Ho.

Noon Lane

Lane

13-18

Boundary Lane

Causeway End

Black Moor

Stalks Ho.

Mawdesley (Chapel)

Lathom W.M.

Black Moor Houses

Burscough Moss

Meadow Lane

Prescot Bridge

Baldwins Br.

Back Lane

Bentley

Greens Tit

Snipe Hall

Carters

Bispham Green

Brook Bent

Back Moss Lane

Wilbrahans Meadows

Hall

Bispham

Moss Lane

Eller Brook

St Johns Chapelry

Days Green

Warpers Moss

New Sitch Ho.

Horscear

Moss

Wanes Blades Bridge

Low Meadows

Grimshaw Green

School

Peak Ho.

Barn

79

Old Sitch Ho.

Robyn Lane

Runnel Brow

Br.

New Barn

Tawd Side

Fairhurst Farm

Cross

Brinscall Brow

The Hall

Top Locks

Car Hall

Mawkinhurst

Eves Lane

Common Ho.

Dover Bridge

Ollertons

Frog Lane

Scarisbrick Farm

Tan Parbold

Br.

Mill

Ring o Bells

Ivy Ho.

River Tawd

Lane Ho.

Burscough

Briars Hall

Bridge

Black Moss Br.

Spencers Br.

Giants Hall

8

27

R.C.Chapel

Three Oaks

Carlings

26

Ivy Ho.

Newburgh

Burscough Hall

Lowry Hill

Course

Lovers Bridge

Tabby Nook

Brow

School

Brook

Langleys

Lathom Row

Lane

Berry Farm

Water View

Round Thorn

Lawrensons

Woodcock Ho.

Holcroft

Blythe

Cottage

Hall Lane

The Bell

Rigmaidens

Pug Ho.

Dalton Common

Needless Inn

Preston Lodges

Park

Newburgh Lodge

Wood

Lows

Mount Pleasant

Blythe Lane

Abbey

Lathom

Hillocks

Cranes Lane

New Park

Dairy

Deer Park

Bows Barn

Delph

School

New Park Wood

Halsalls Lodge

Temple Wood

Moss Ho.

The Grange

Ashton

Hall

Brook

Rough

1   2

1 mile approx.

Published 1840 - 1844.

◁81

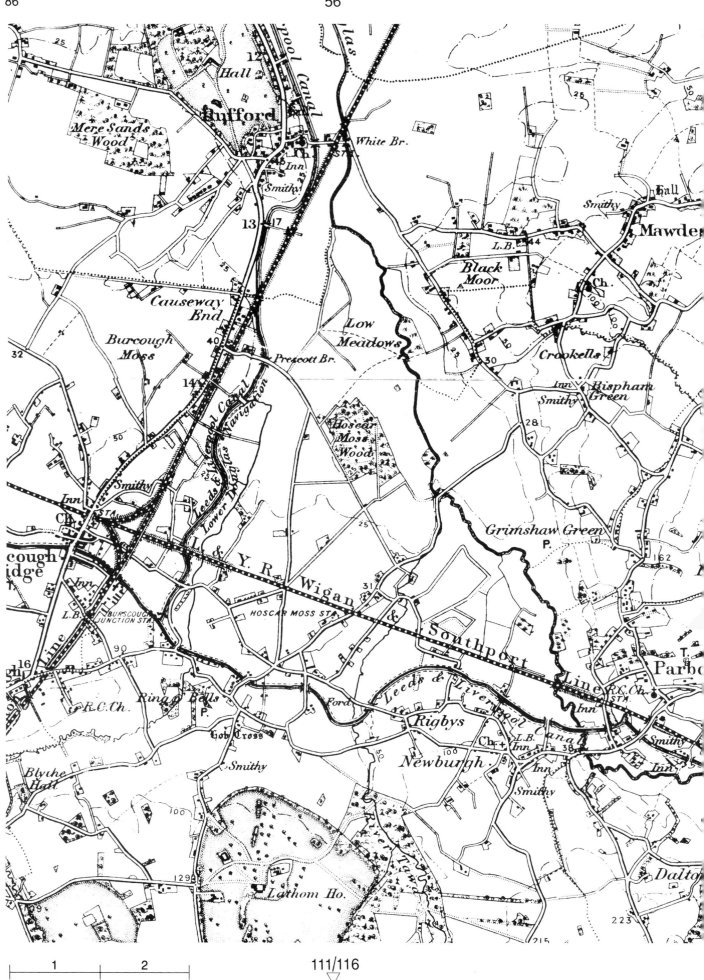

1   2

1 mile approx.

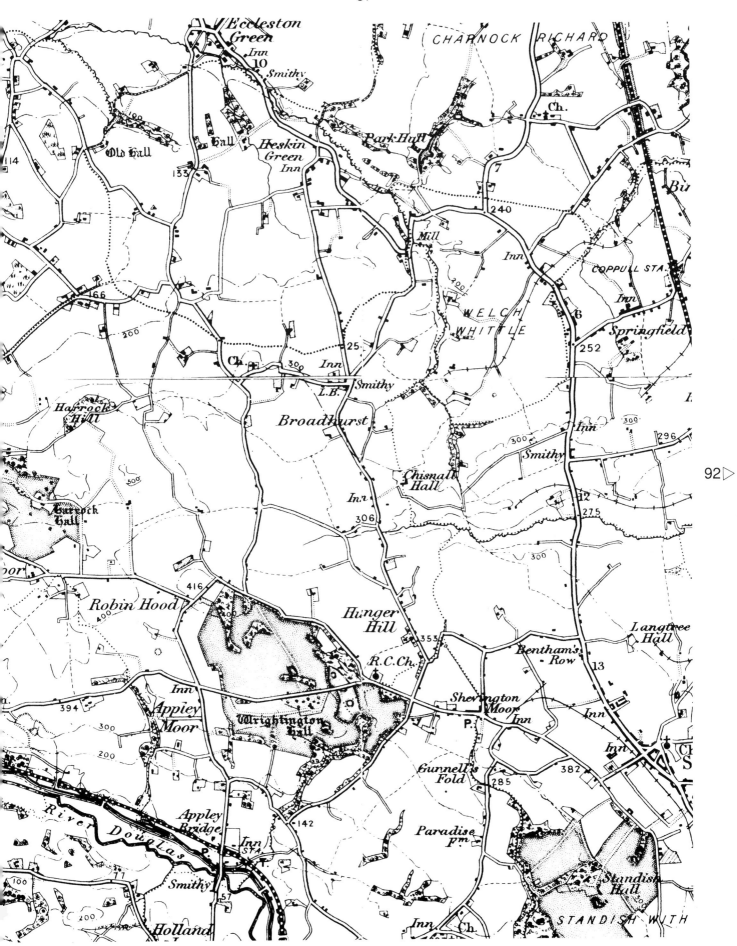

Surveyed 1889 - 93. Revised 1892 / 5. Published 1896.

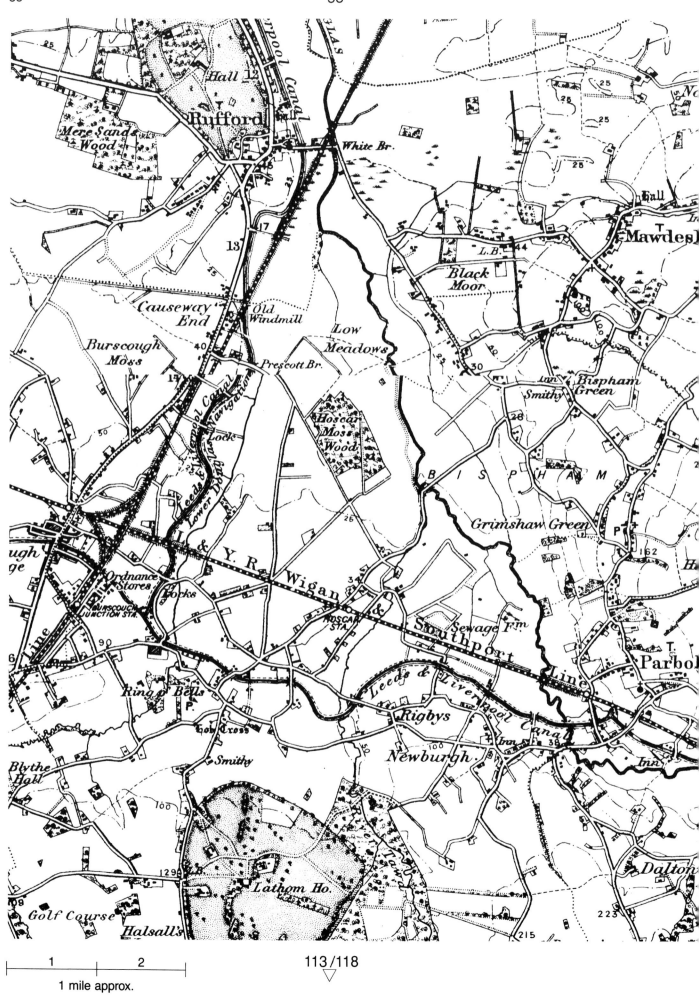

Hall 12

Rufford

Mere Sands
Wood

White Br.

Mawdesl

L.B.

Black
Moor

Causeway
End

Old
Windmill

Low
Meadows

Burscough
Moss

Prescott Br.

Inn

Smithy

Bispham
Green

Hoscar
Moss
Wood

B

I S P H A M

Lock

Grimshaw Green

P

Ordnance
Stores

L. & Y. R.

Wigan

&

Southport

Line

Forks

BURSCOUGH
JUNCTION STA.

HOSCAR
STA.

Sewage Fm

Parbo

ugh
ge

Ring o' Bells
P.

Rigbys

Leeds & Liverpool Canal

Inn

Inn

Bob Cross

Newburgh

Blythe
Hall

Smithy

Dalton

Golf Course

Lathom Ho.

Halsall's

1   2

1 mile approx.

Surveyed 1844 - 47 / 1888 - 93. Revised 1910 - 12. Published 1912 - 13.

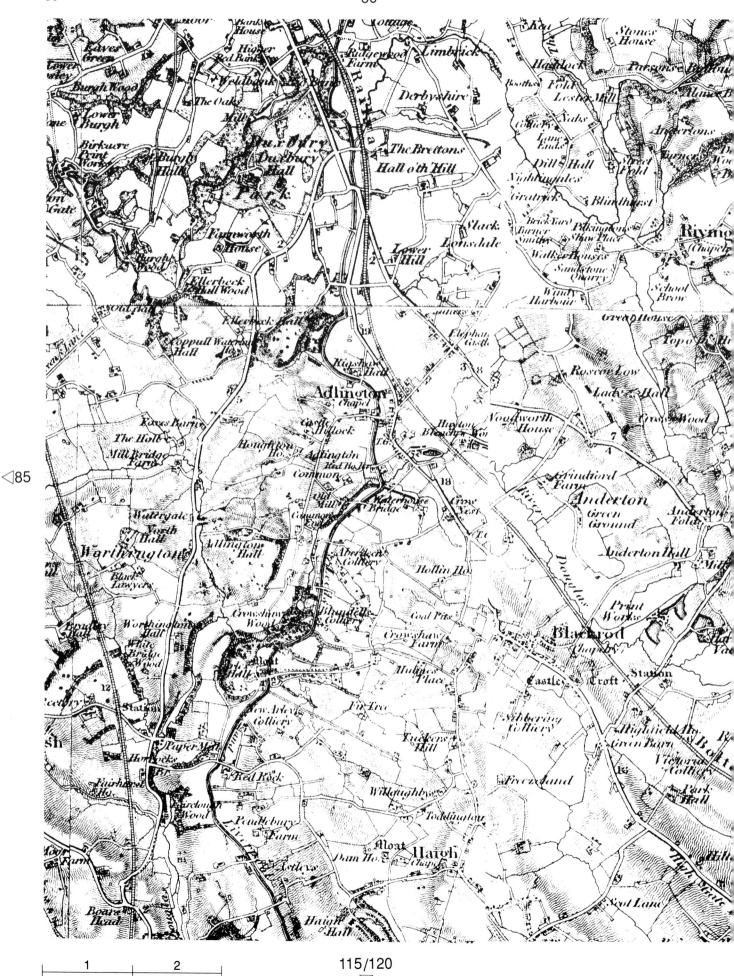

1

2

1 mile approx.

Published 1840 - 1844.

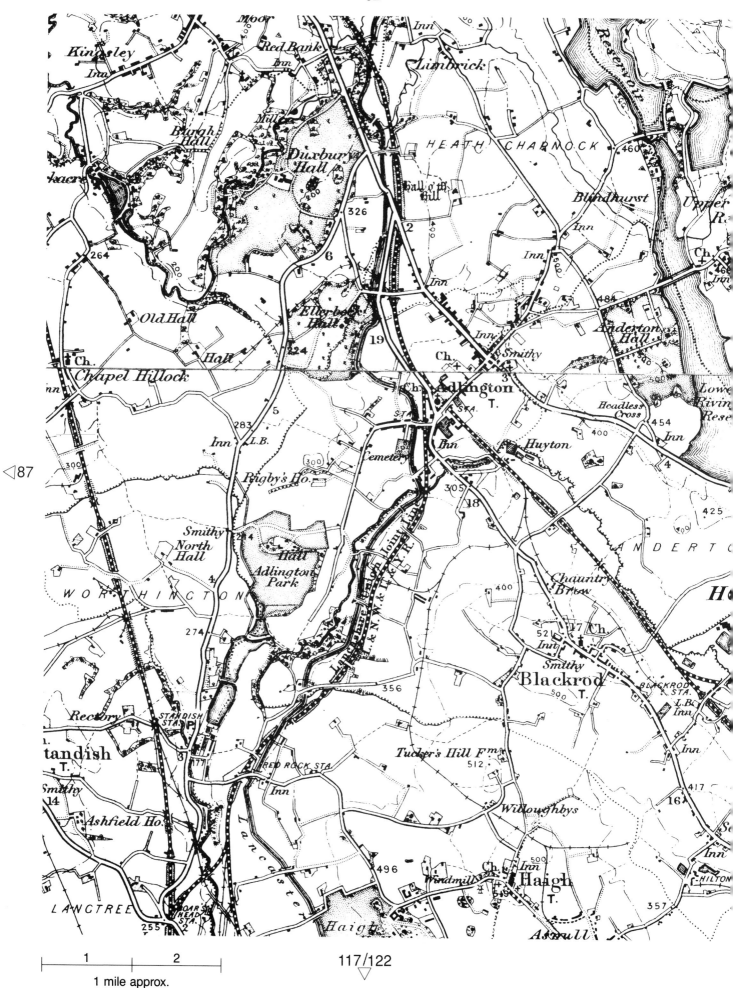

1   2

1 mile approx.

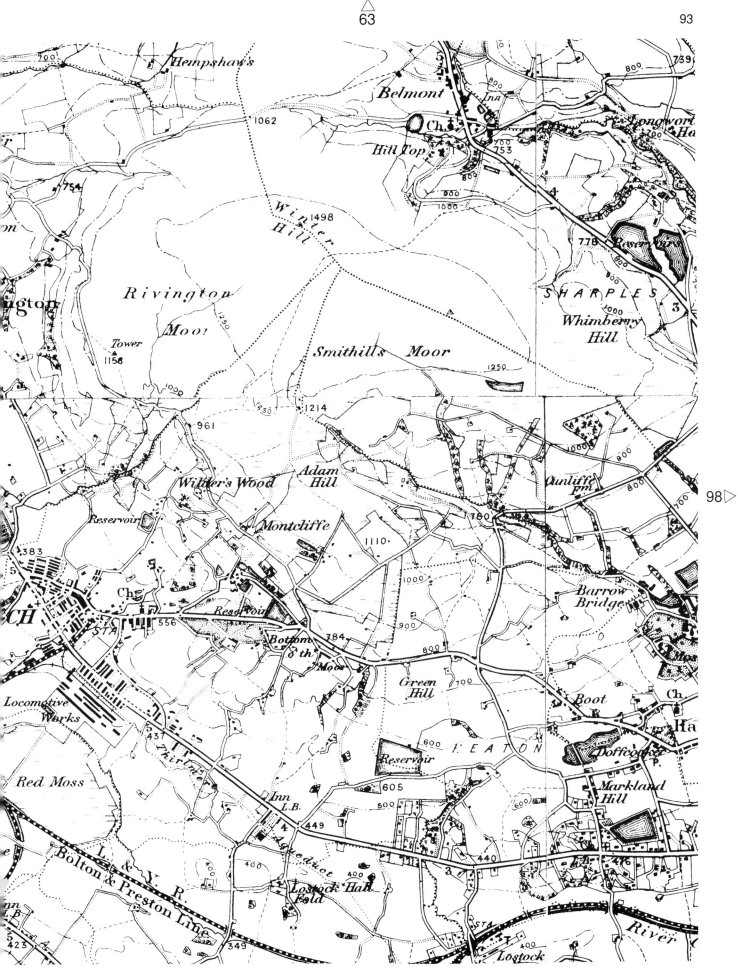

Surveyed 1889 - 93. Revised 1892 / 5. Published 1896.

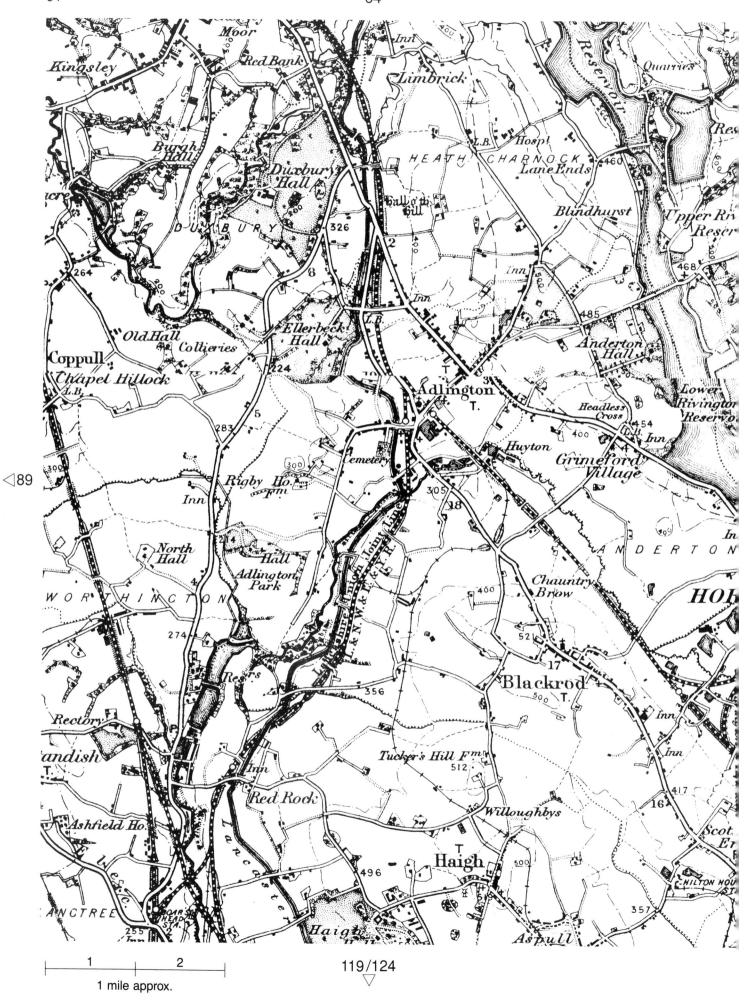

Kingsley

Moor

Red Bank

Limbrick

Burgh Hall

Duxbury Hall

HEATH CHARNOCK
Lane Ends

L.B.
Hosp.

Blindhurst

Upper R.
Reser

Quarries

Res

DUXBURY

326

Gallagh
Hill

2

Inn

Inn

Inn

Inn

468

Old Hall

Collieries

Ellerbeck
Hall

L.B.

485

Anderton
Hall

Coppull

224

Lower
Rivington
Reservo

Chapel Hillock

L.B.

Adlington

T

T

Headless
Cross

454

L.B. Inn

△89

283

5

Cemetery

Huyton

400

Grimeford
Village

300

Rigby Ho.
Fm.

305

Inn

18

North
Hall

Hall

Adlington
Park

ANDERTON

HO

W O R T H I N G T O N

274

Chauntry
Brow

460

52

HOLL

356

17

Blackrod

500

T

Rectory

Inn

andish

T

Tucker's Hill Fm.

512

Inn

Red Rock

417

Ashfield Ho.

Inn

Willoughbys

16

Scot
En

Lancaster

T
Haigh

500

496

HILTON HOU
ST

255

ANCTREE

OARS
HEAD
STA

Haigh

Aspull

357

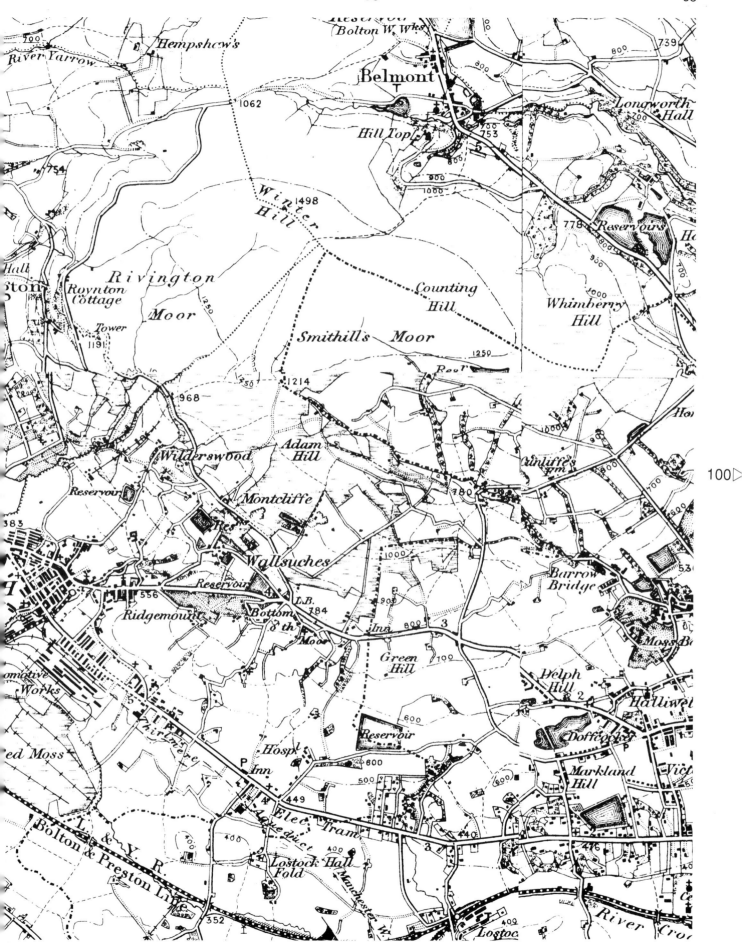

100▷

125

Surveyed 1844 - 47 / 1888 - 93. Revised 1910 - 12. Published 1912 - 13.

1   2

1 mile approx.

Published 1840 - 1844.

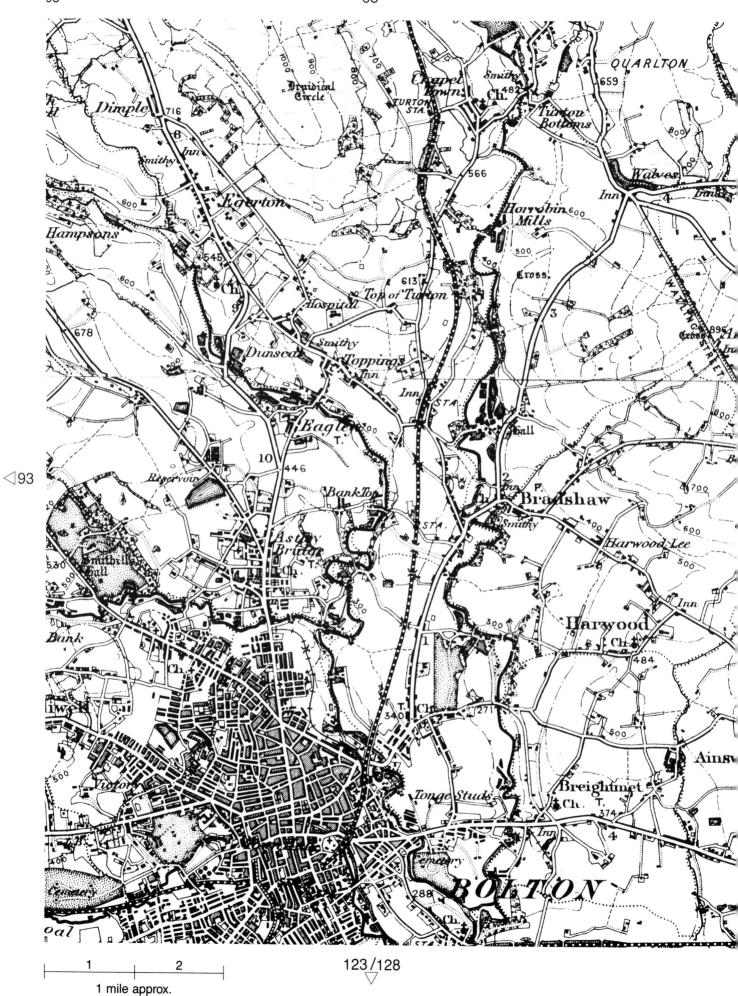

QUARLTON

659

Smithy 482

Chapel Town Ch.

Turton Bottoms

TURTON STA.

800

Walves

Inn 4

Dimple 716

8 Smithy Inn

Egerton 566

Horrobin Mills 600

500

Cross.

Hampsons 545

600 Ch.

678 Hospital

613

Top of Turton Ch.

3 WATLING STREET 895

Smithy

Dunscar Toppings Inn

STA.

Inn

◁93

Reservoir

Eagley T.

10 446 BankTop

STA.

Hall 700

2 Inn P.

Bradshaw

400

Harwood Lee 500

500

Smithy Hall

Astley Bridge Ch. T.

300

300

Inn

Harwood Ch. 484

Bank

Ch.

500

1

T. Ch. 340 271

500

Ainsw

Yarton 500

Breightmet Ch. T. 374

Tonge Studs

BOLTON 4

100 B.

288 Ch.

Cemetery

oal

1   2

1 mile approx.

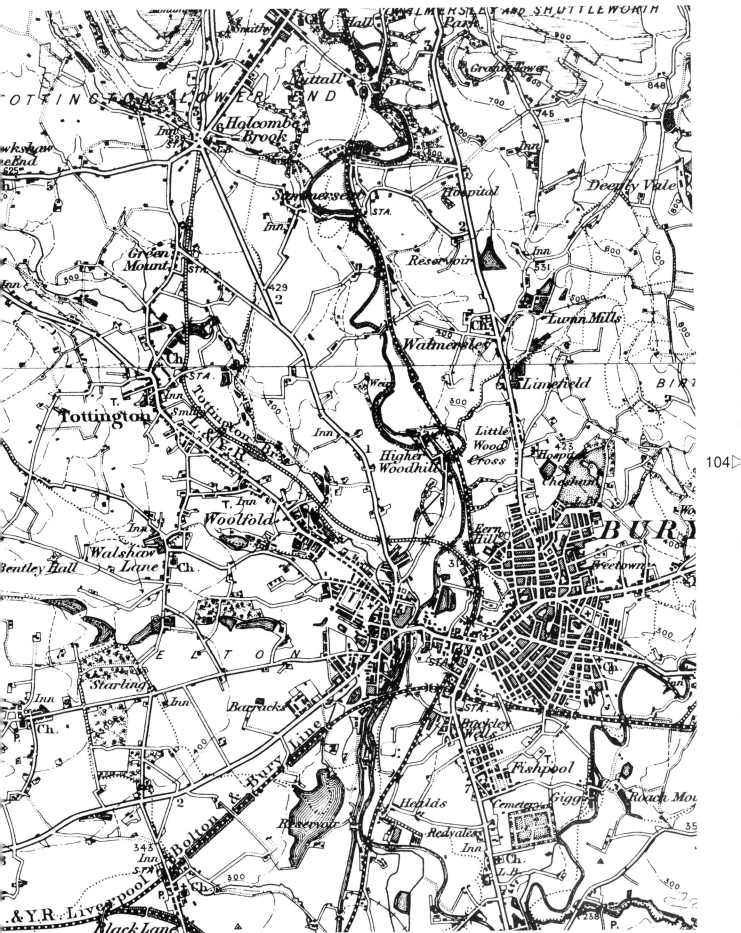

104▷

Surveyed 1847 - 49. Revised 1895. Published 1896.

5

Dimple
716
Hall
Smithy Inn

Draidical
Circle

Chapel
Town

482
T
659

Turton
Bottoms

Turton
800

4
Egerton
600

Turton Tower
566

Horrobin
Mills (Bleach)
600
Reservoir
Inn

Brook
500
4

impsons
545

L.B.
613
Top of Turton
Cross.
The Grange
896
Cross
Affe

678
Hospital
Dunscar
Smithy
Toppings
Bradshaw
Bromley
Cross
WATLING STREET WATLING

rocks Fold
Eagley
T
T
Inn
BROMLEY CROSS
STA.
all
800

Les Tram
446
700
Side of the
Moor
Bows
Hi

Reservoir
Bank Top
Bradshaw
Inn
P
700
Harwood
Lee
400
600

Smithill
Hall
THE OAKS
STA.
Ruins
500
Inn

800
Hall i'th'Wood
500
L.B.
484

Firwood
Works.
Harwood

Union
Mills
800
Thicketford Br.
271
500

RedBridgeMill
Ainswor
Bleach Wor

Breightmet
T
373
4
Blackshaw Brook

Town Hall
Colliery
Cemetery TongeFold
288
BOLTON

cemetery
Springfield
Bradley Fold

1   2
1 mile approx.

| 1 | 2 |

1 mile approx.

Published 1840 - 1844.

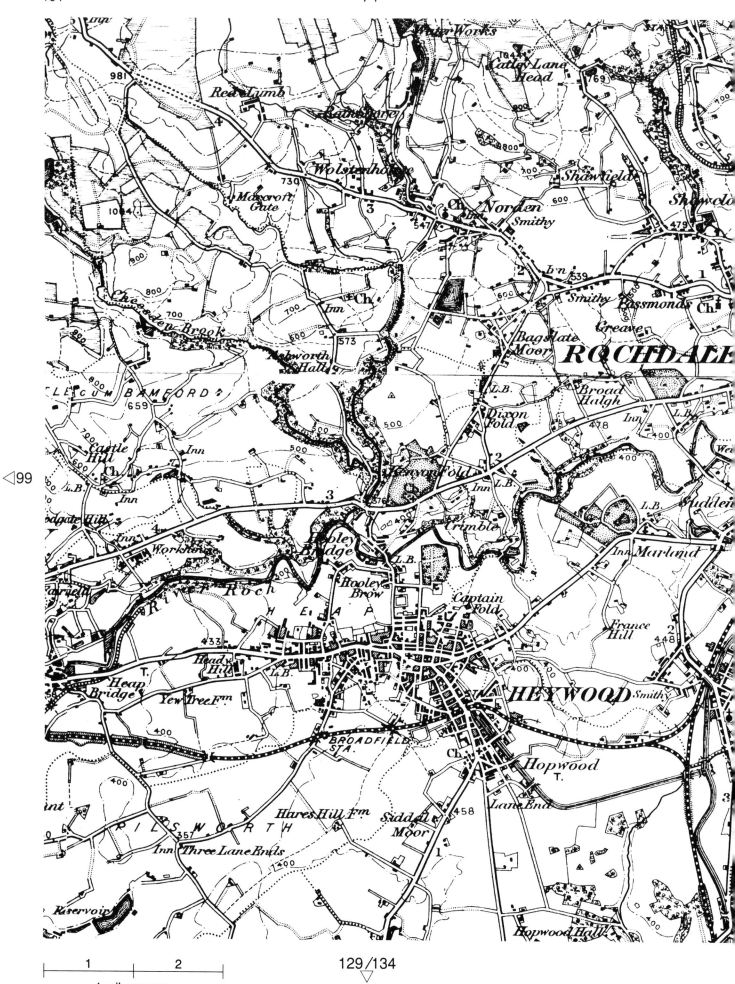

1 mile approx.

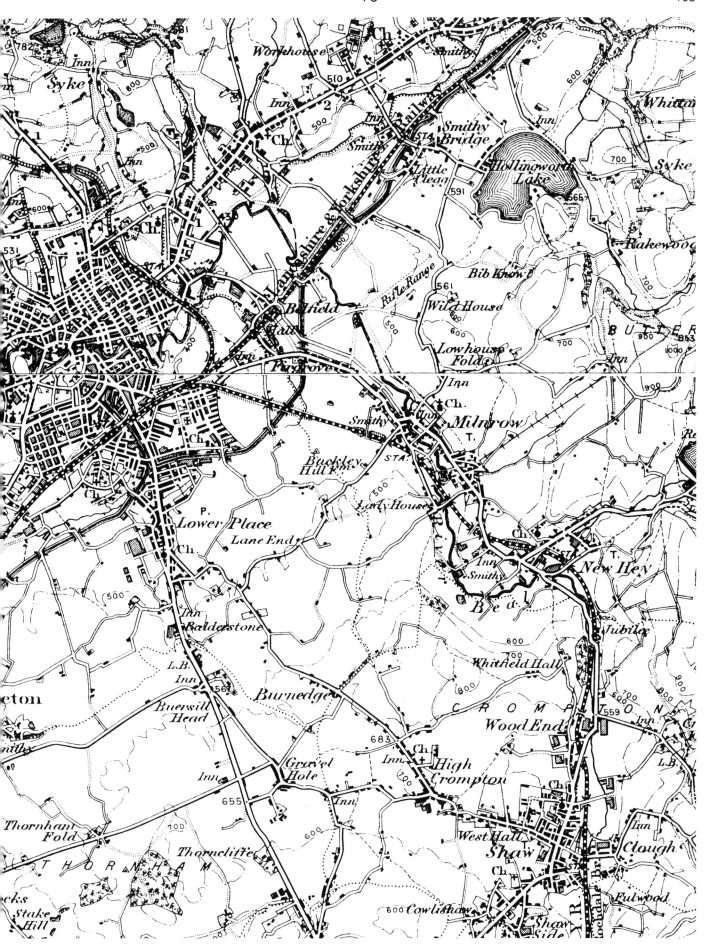

Surveyed 1889 - 92. Revised 1892. Published 1896.

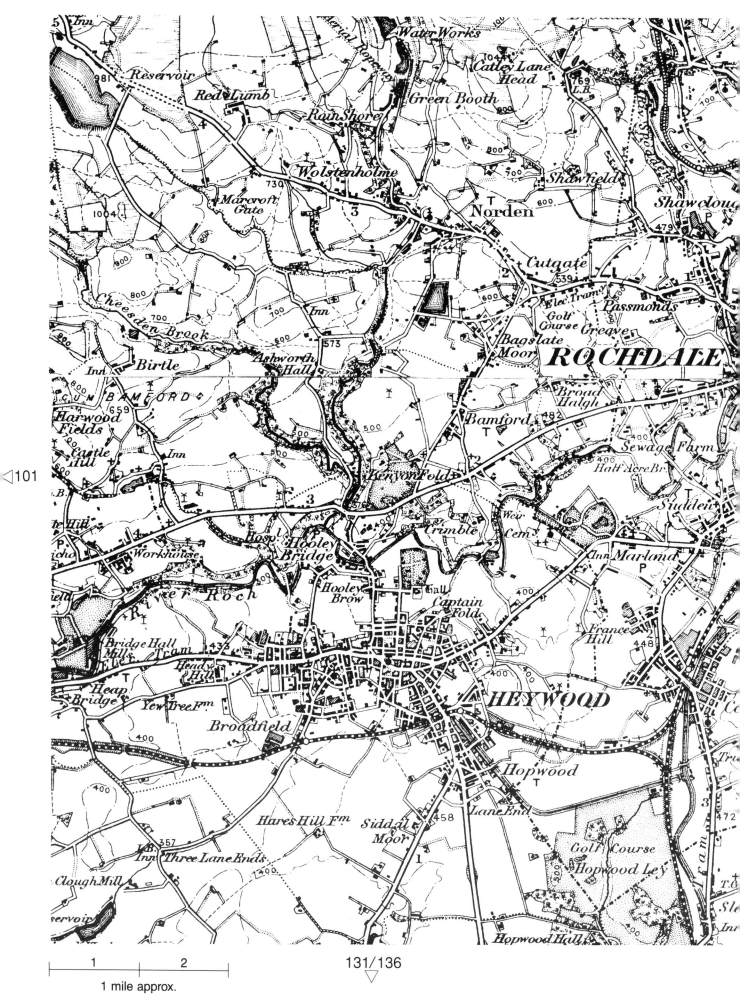

1 mile approx.

Surveyed 1871 - 72. Revised 1911. Published 1913.

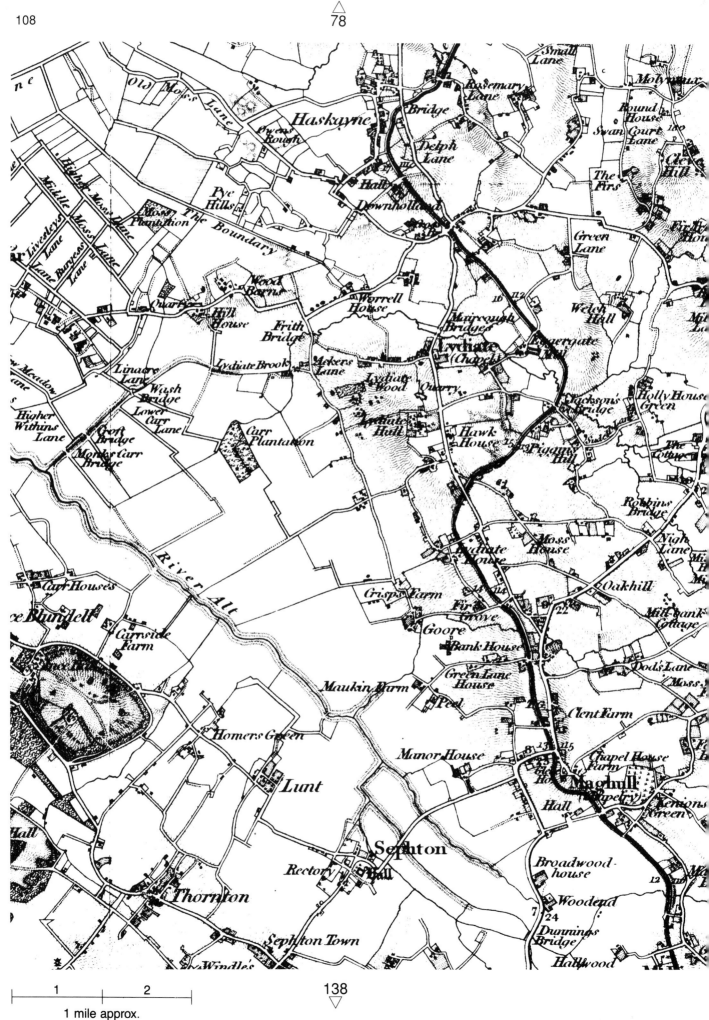

Haskayne

Owens Rough

Old Moss Lane

Pye Hills

The Boundary

Moss Plantation

Wood Barns

Hall

Downholland

Bridge

Delph Lane

Rosemary Lane

Small Lane

Molyneux

Round House

Swan Court Lane

The Firs

Cleg Hill

Firs Ho.

Green Lane

Welch Hall

Middle Moss Lane

Higher Moss Lane

Liveleys Lane

Burgess Lane

Lane

Quarry

Hill House

Frith Bridge

Worrell House

Maircough Bridge

Lydiate Chapel)

Sergate Hall

Lydiate Brook

Ackers Lane

Lydiate Wood

Quarry

Jackson's Bridge

Holly House Green

New Meadow Lane

Linacre Lane

Wash Bridge

Lower Carr Lane

Lydiate Hall

Hawk House

Pigans Hill

The Cottage

Higher Withins Lane

Goft Bridge

Monks Carr Bridge

Carr Plantation

Robbins Bridge

Night Lane

ce Blundell

River Alt

Carr Houses

Lydiate House

Moss House

Oakhill

Carrside Farm

Grisps Farm

Fir Grove

Bank House

Mill Bank Cottage

Dod's Lane

Moss

Goore

Green Lane House

Clent Farm

Homers Green

Maukin Farm

Peel

Manor House

Chapel House Farm

Lunt

Hall

Broadwood-house

Woodend

Sephton

Rectory

Hall

Sephton Town

Thornton

Windle's

Dunnings Bridge

Hallwood

1   2

1 mile approx.

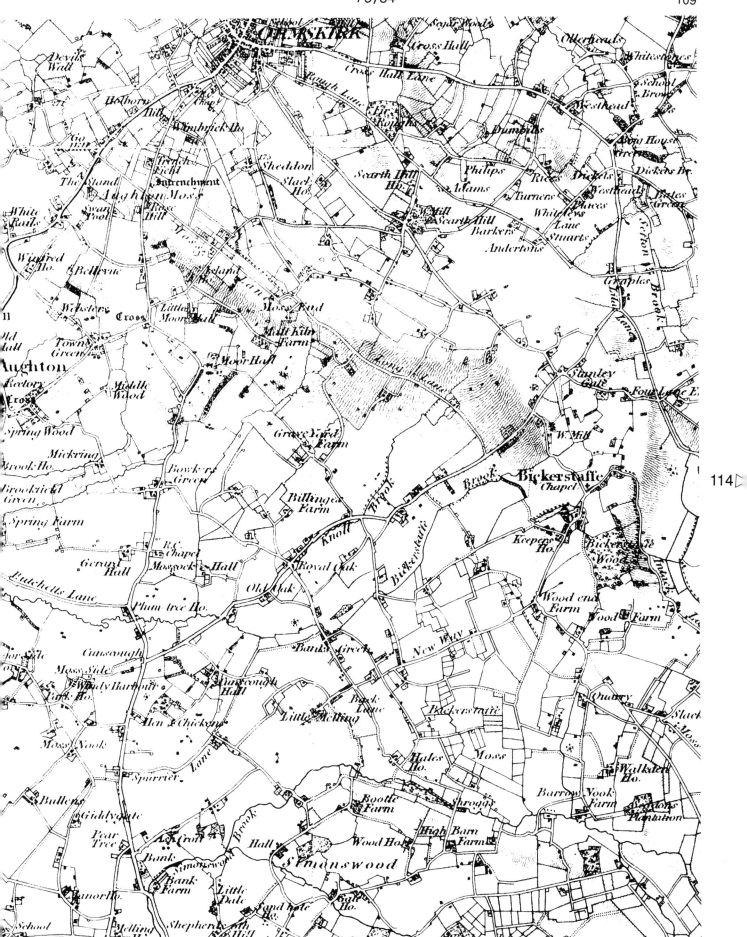

114 ▷

Published 1840 - 1844.

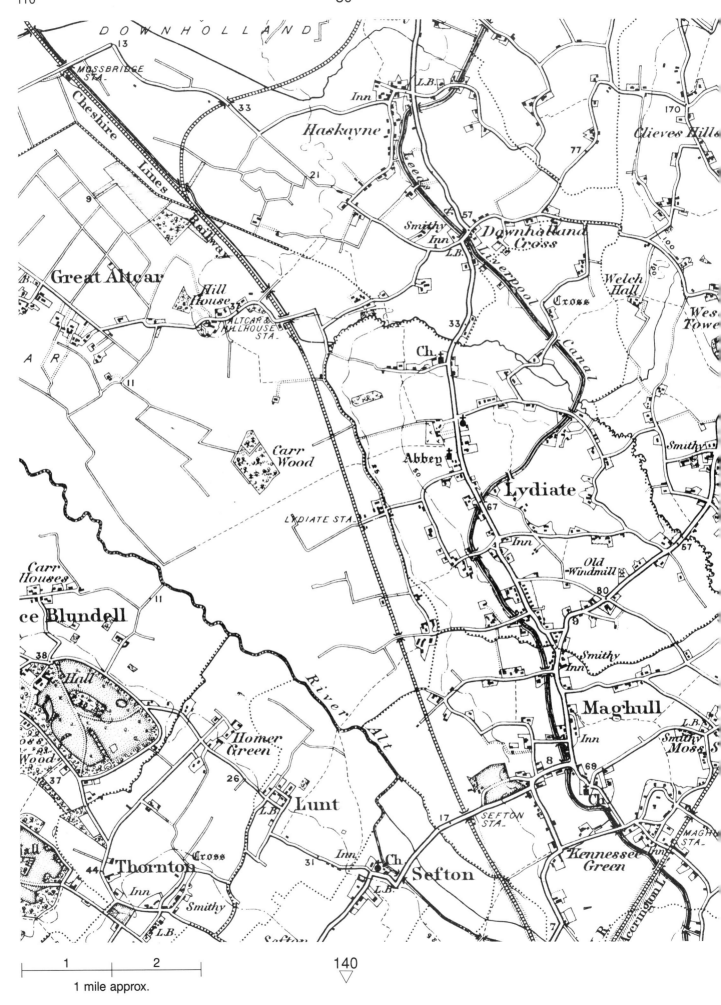

1 mile approx.

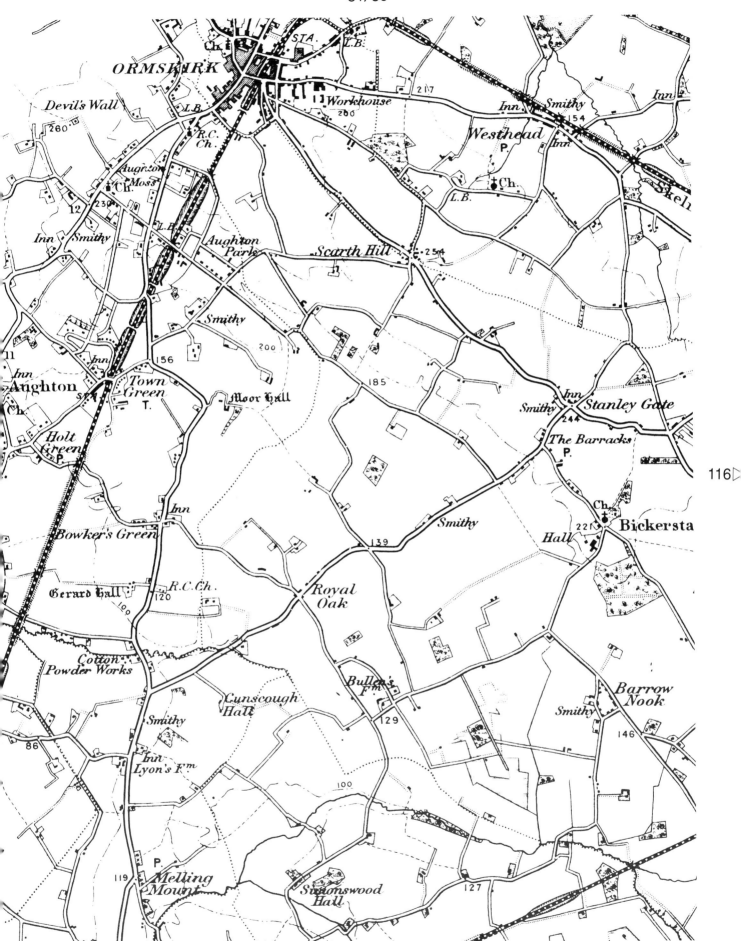

ORMSKIRK

Devil's Wall

260

Aughton
Moss
Ch.

12 230

Inn Smithy

11

Inn
Aughton
Ch.

ST.A.

Holt
Green
P

Bowker's Green

Gerard Hall

100
120

R.C.Ch.

Cotton
Powder Works

Smithy
Inn
Lyon's Fm

86

119

Melling
Mount
P

STA.
Ch.
L.B.

L.B.

R.C.
Ch.

Aughton
Park

Smithy

Town
Green
T.

156

200

Moor Hall

Inn

Workhouse
260

Scarth Hill

185

139

Royal
Oak

Cunscough
Hall

Bullen's
Fm

129

100

Suttonswood
Hall

217

Westhead
P

Ch.

L.B.

254

Smithy

Smithy

Smithy

Inn Smithy
154

Inn

Skeh

Inn
Stanley Gate
244

The Barracks
P

116

Ch.
221 Bickersta

Hall

Barrow
Nook
Smithy
146

127

Surveyed 1869 - 74 / 1889 - 92. Revised 1892 - 95. Published 1896.

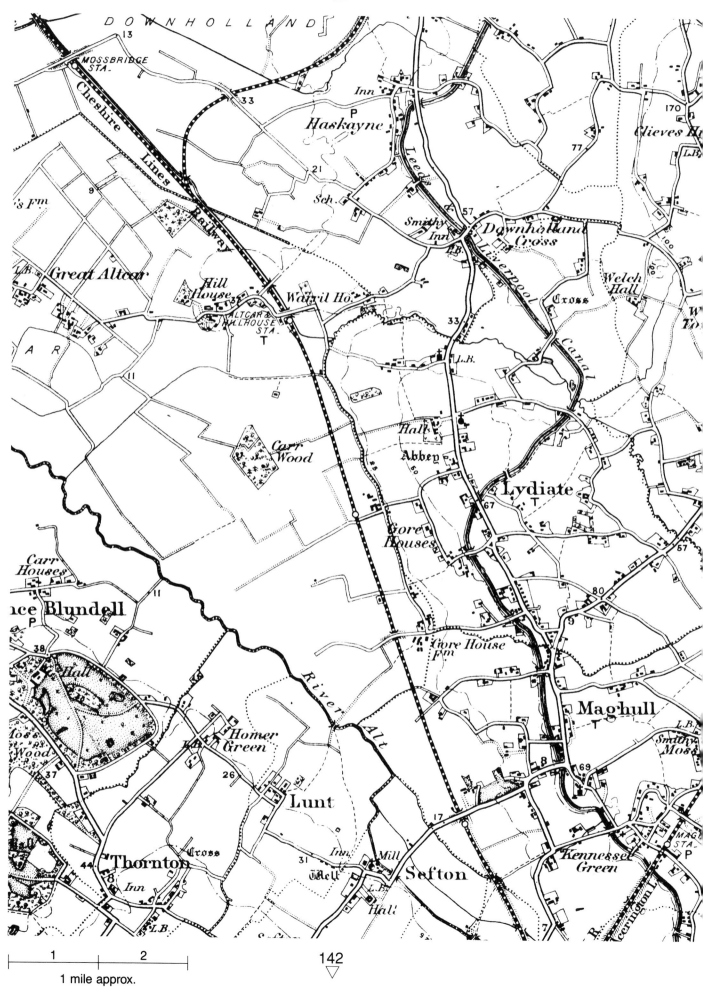

1   2

1 mile approx.

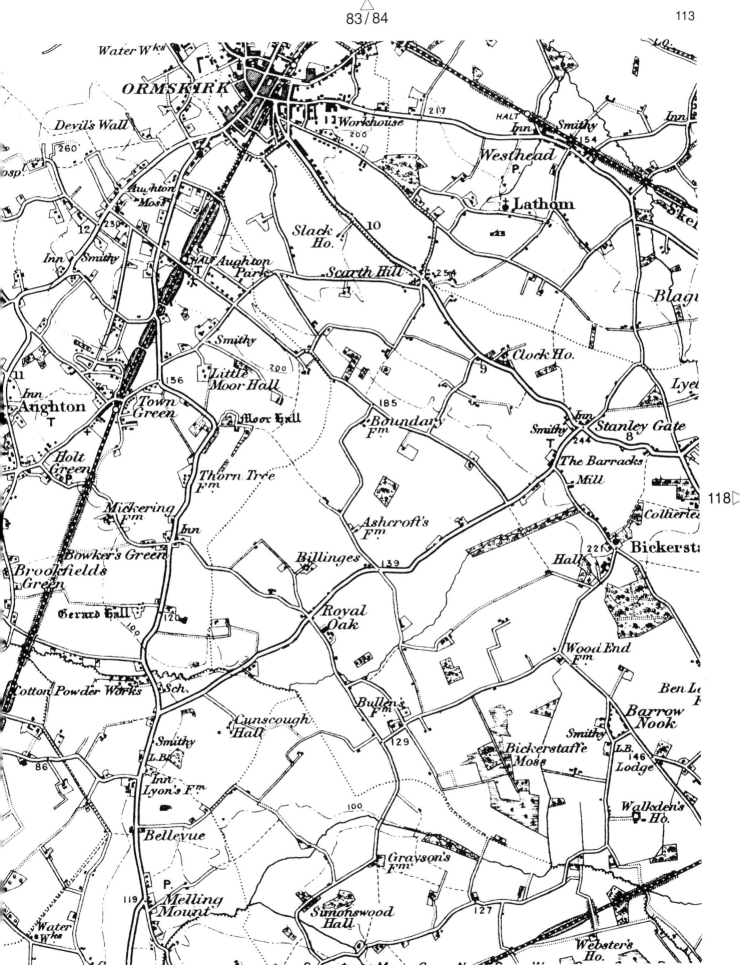

Surveyed 1844 - 47. Revised 1910. Published 1912.

◁109

1   2

1 mile approx.

Published 1840 - 1844.

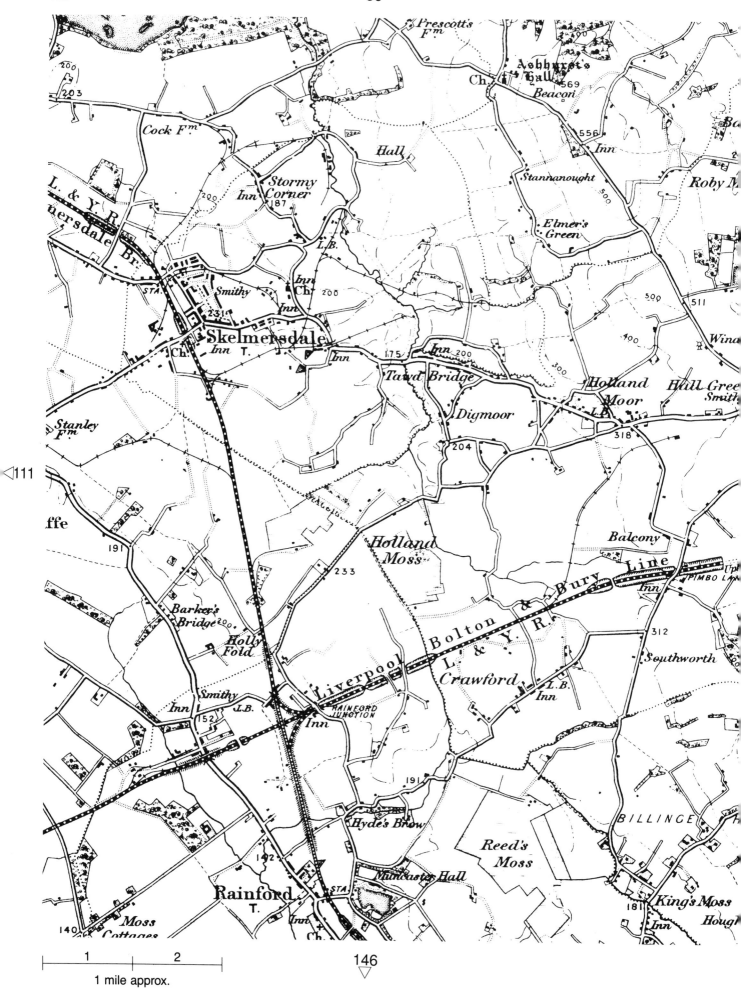

△111

1

2

1 mile approx.

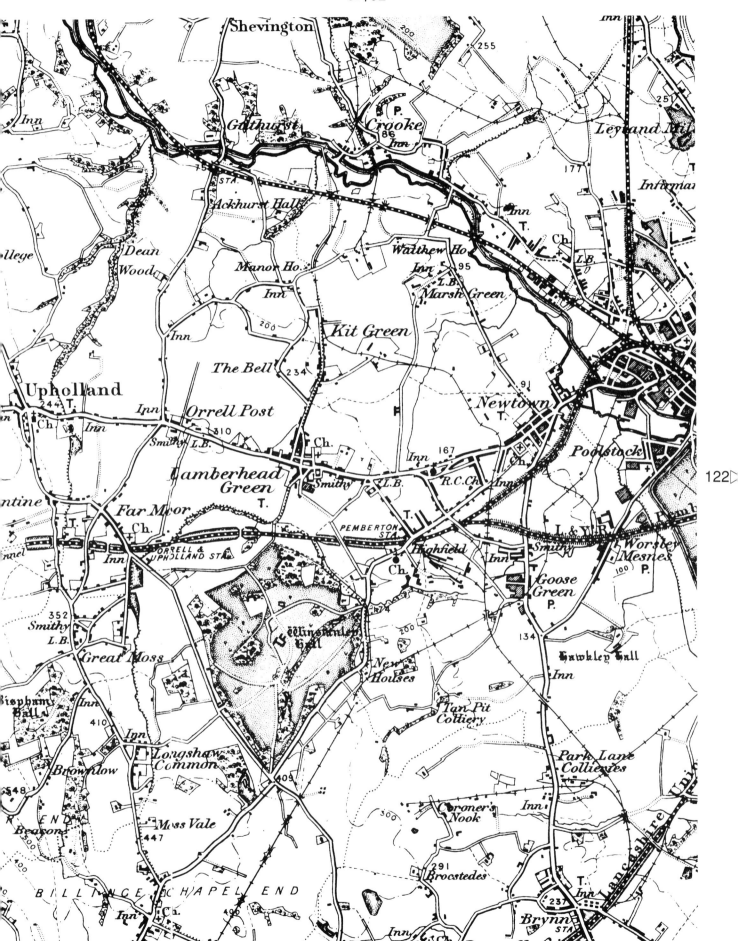

Surveyed 1869 - 74 / 1889 - 92. Revised 1892 - 95. Published 1896.

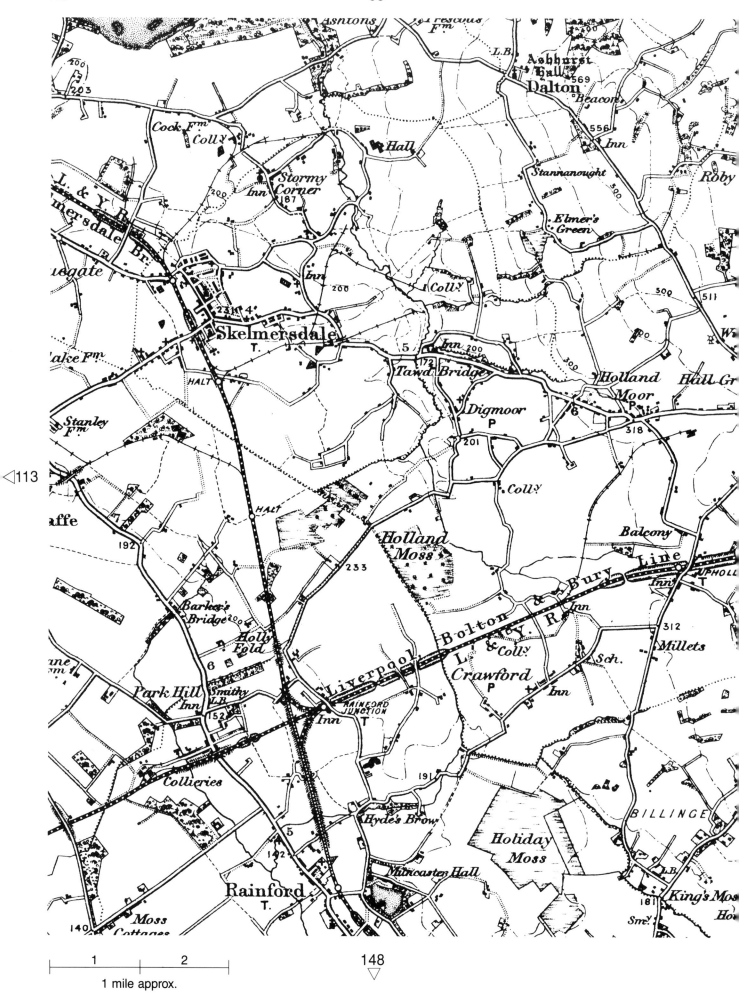

◁113

148
▽

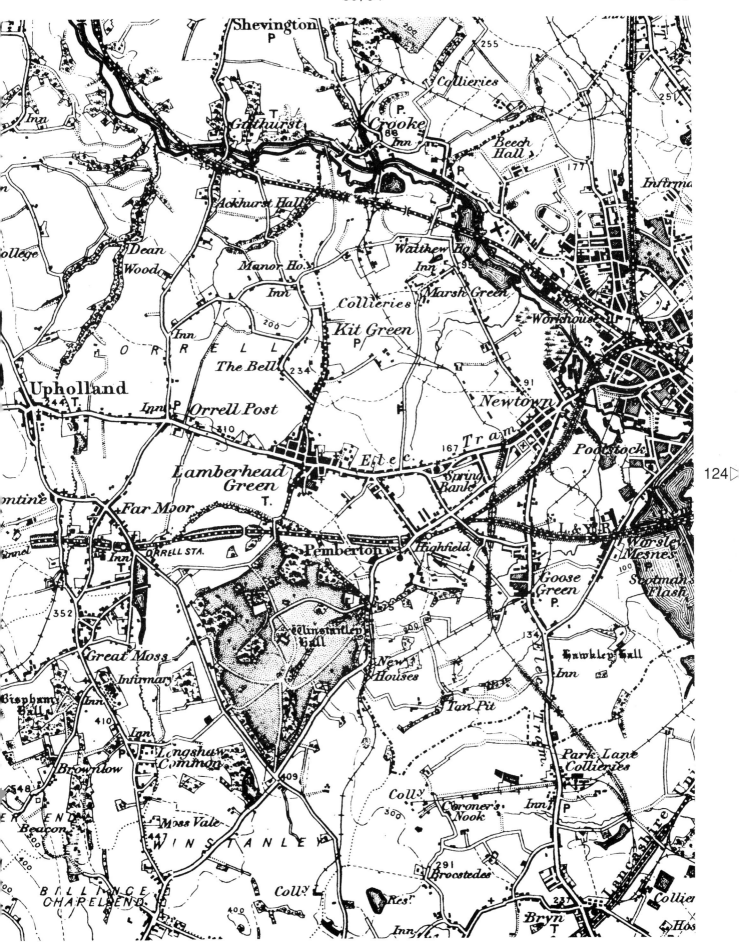

Shevington
P

Collieries
255
P.
Gathurst
T
Crooke
Inn
86
Collieries
Beech
Hall
P
251
Ackhurst Hall
Infirma
Walthew Ho.
Inn
Dean
Wood
Marsh Green
Manor Ho.
Collieries
Workhouse
Inn
Kit Green
P
Inn
The Bell 234
200
Newtown
91
Upholland
Inn
P
Orrell Post
Pootstock
244 T
310
124
Elec. Tram
167
Lamberhead
Green
Spring
Banks
L & Y R.
Worsley
Mesnes
Far Moor
T
Worsley
Mesnes
ORRELL STA.
100
Pemberton
Highfield
P
Goose
Green
P
Scotman's
Flash
134
352
Winstanley
Hall
Hawkley Hall
Inn
Great Moss
New
Houses
Infirmary
Tan Pit
Bispham
Hall
Inn
Park Lane
Collieries
Inn
P
410
Longshaw
Common
P
Brownlow
409
Colly
Inn
P
548
Coroner's
Nook
300
Beacon
Moss Vale
WINSTANLEY
291
Brocstedes
Coll?
Res.
237
BILLINGE
CHAPEL END.
400
Bryn
T
Hos
Colli

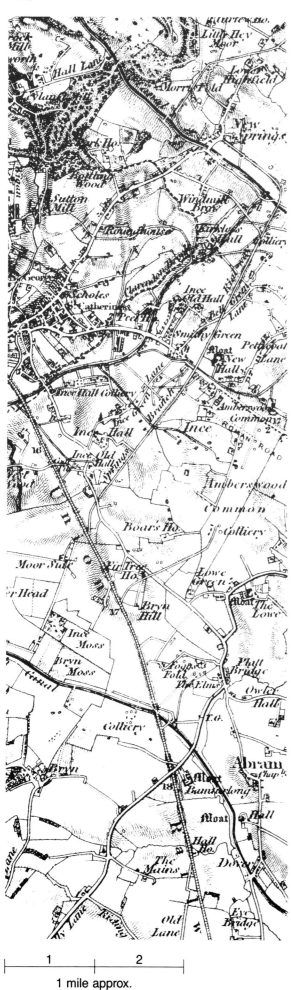

◁115

1   2

1 mile approx.

Published 1840 - 1844.

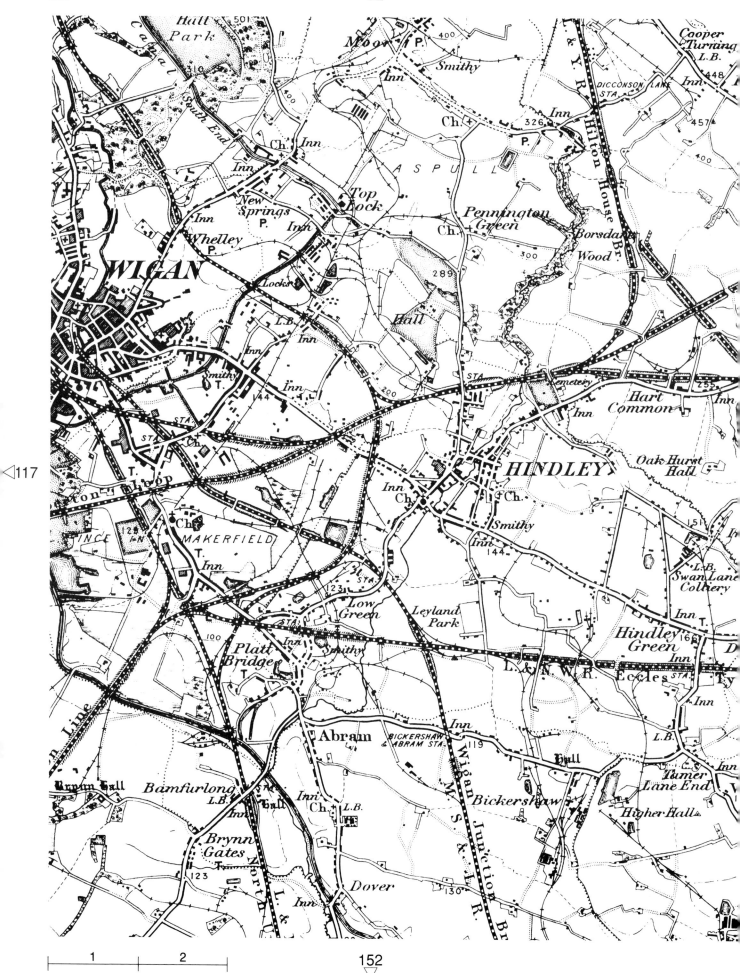

1 mile approx.

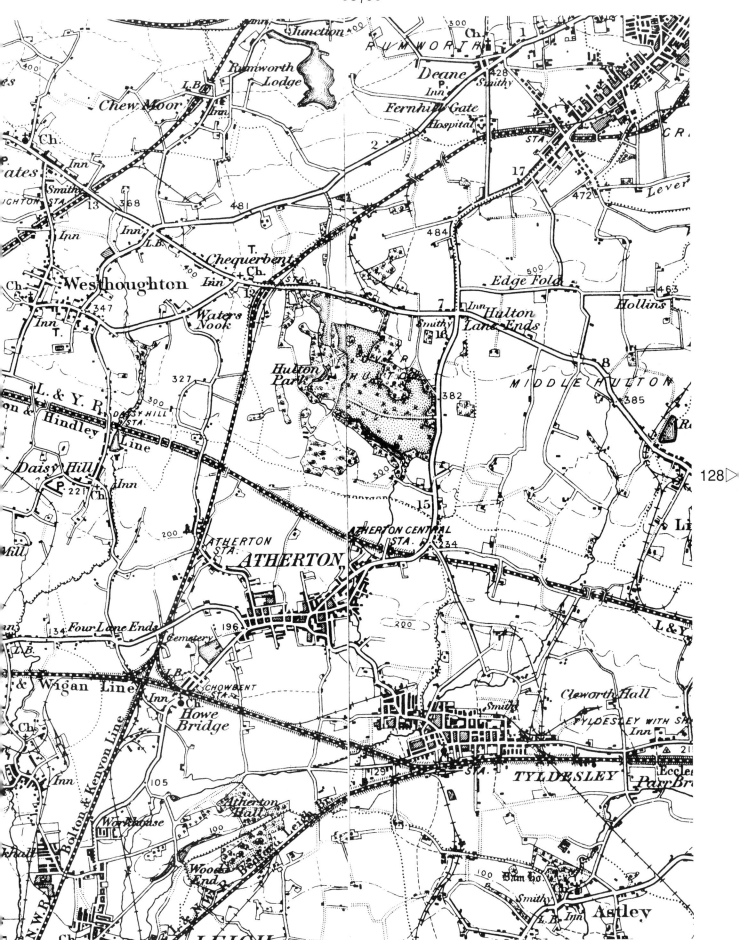

128 ▷

153

Surveyed 1869 - 74 / 1889 - 92. Revised 1892 - 95. Published 1896.

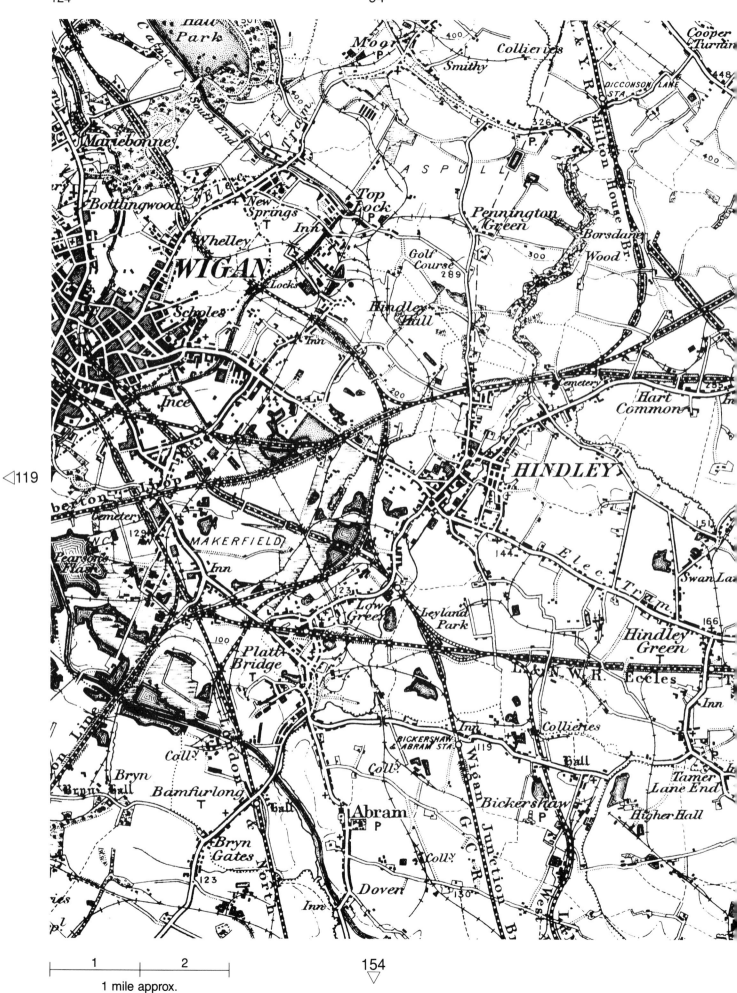

1 mile approx.

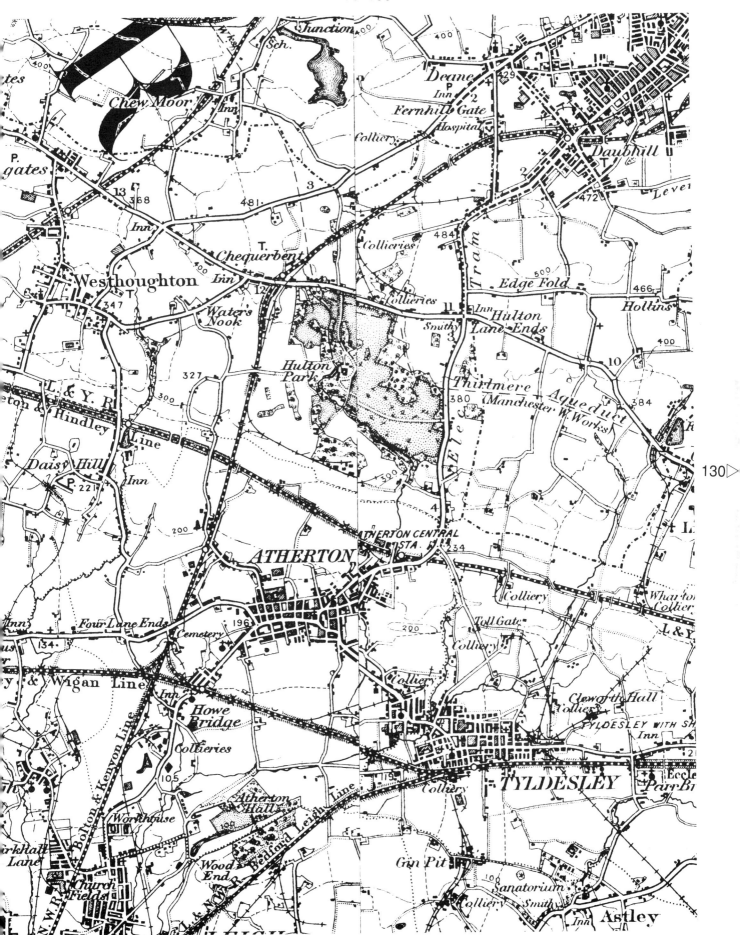

Surveyed 1844 - 47. Revised 1910. Published 1912.

1 mile approx.

Published 1840 - 1844.

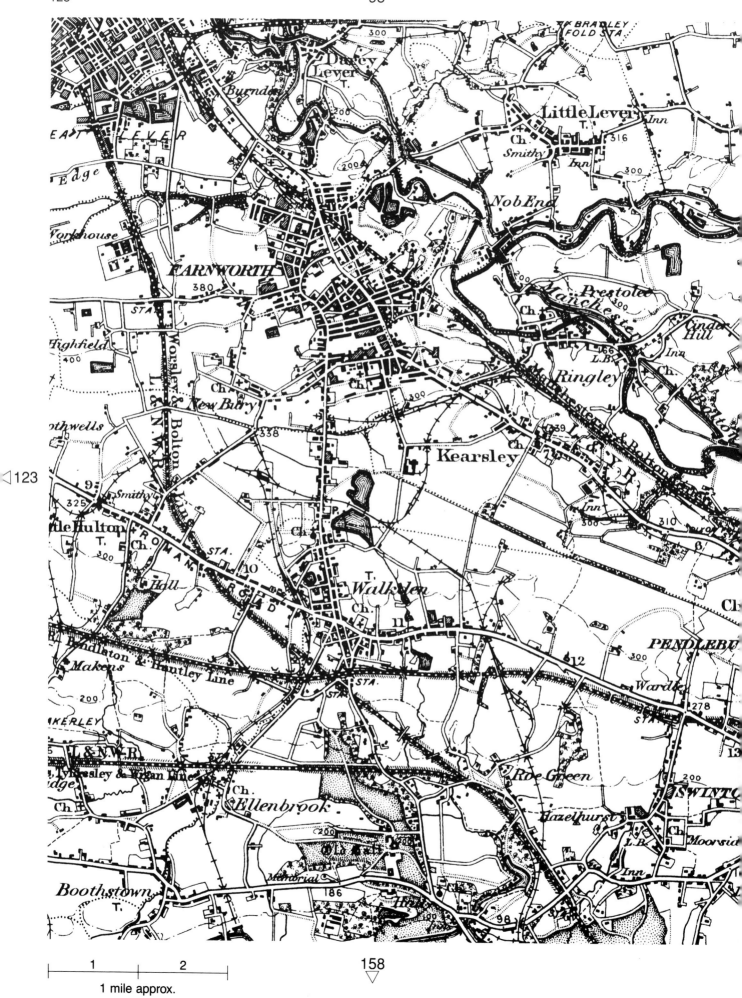

Darcy
Lever
T.

Burnden

LittleLever
T.
Inn

EAST LEVER

Ch.

Smithy
Inn
300

Edge

NobEnd

Workhouse

FARNWORTH
380
STA.

Prestolee
Manchester
Ch.
200
Cinder
Hill
Inn
Ch.

Highfield
400

Ringley
L.B.
166

Ch.
New Bury

Manchester & Bolton
L & Y R.

othwells
338
Ch.
Kearsley
Ch.
139

◁123

9
Smithy
325
Inn
310
300

dleHulton
T.
300
Ch.
R
O
M
A
N
STA.
Ch.
8

Hall
10
Ch.
T.
Walkden
300

Ch.
11
PENDLEBU

yndleston & Hantley Line
STA.
12
300
Wardle
278
STA.

Makens
200
STA.
STA.

KERLEY

L & N W R.

Roe Green
200
SWINTO

Tyldesley & Wigan Line
dge
Ch.
Ch.
Ellenbrook
Hazelhurst
L.B.
Ch.
Moorsi
Inn

Memorial
200

Boothstown
T.
186
Hill
100
98

1   2

1 mile approx.

Surveyed 1871 - 72. Revised 1895. Published 1896.

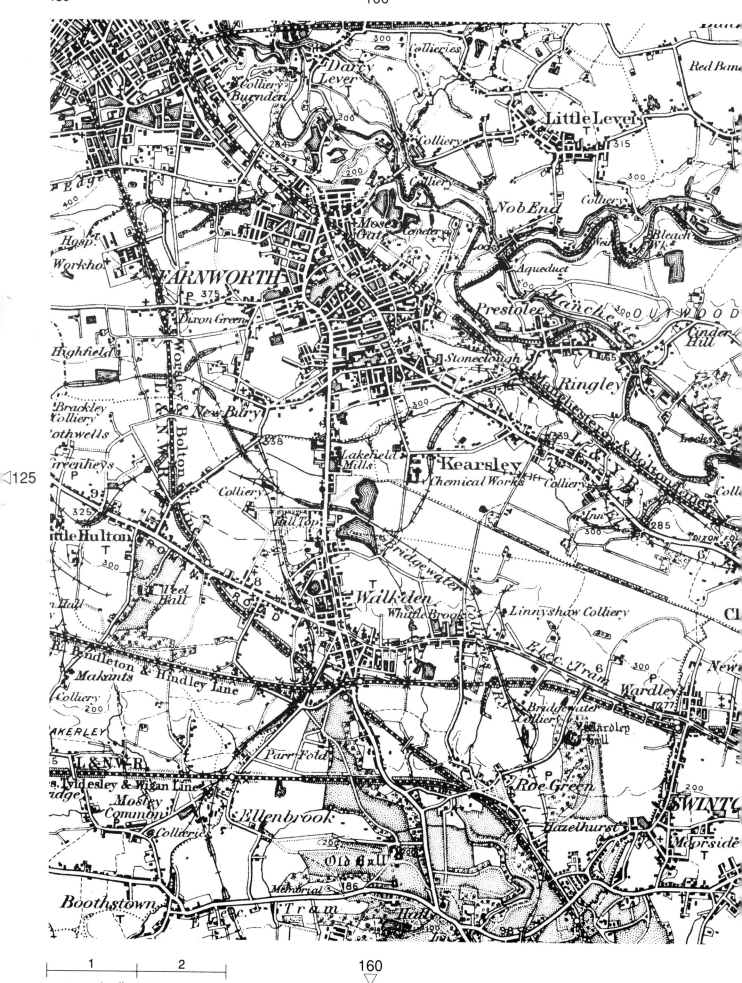

125

160

1

2

1 mile approx.

136 ▷

Surveyed 1844 - 47. Revised 1910. Published 1912.

1

2

1 mile approx.

Published 1840 - 1844.

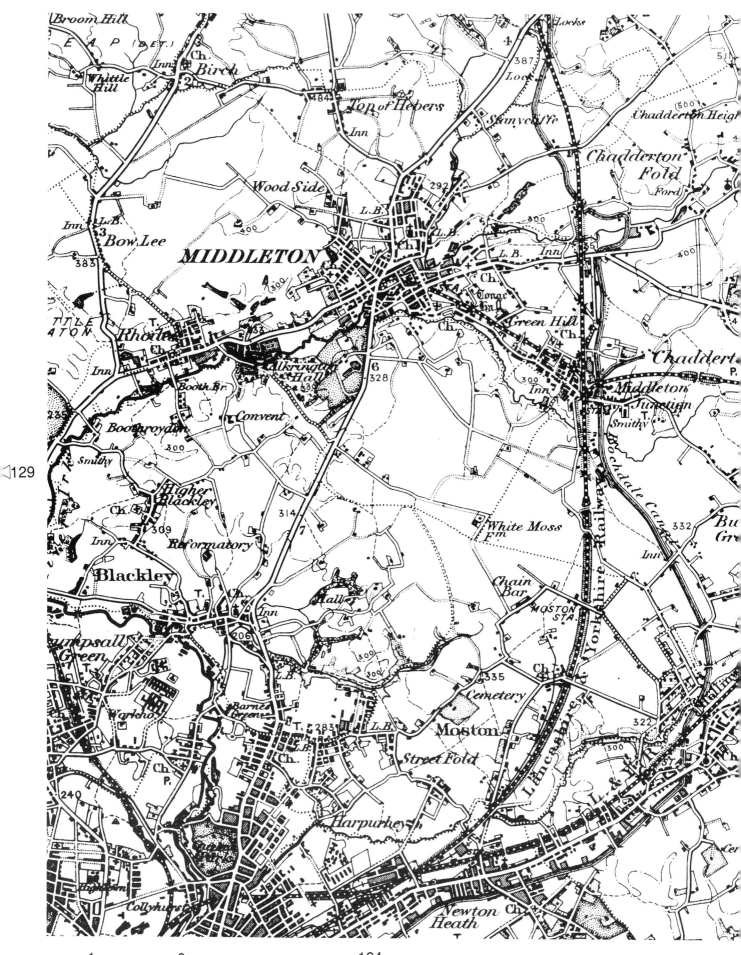

1 mile approx.

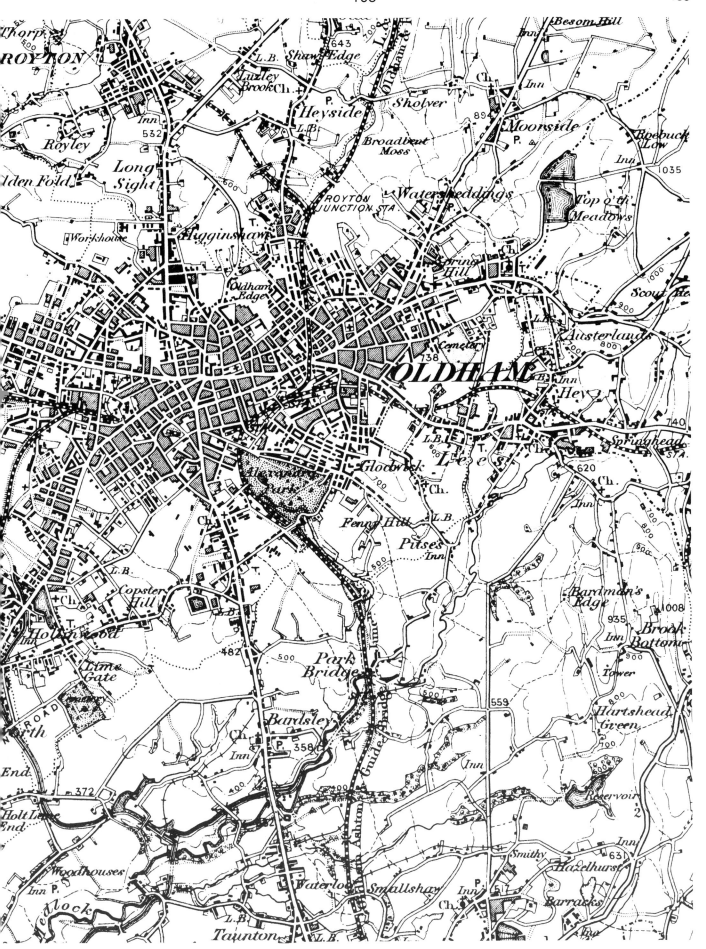

Surveyed 1871 - 72. Revised 1895. Published 1896.

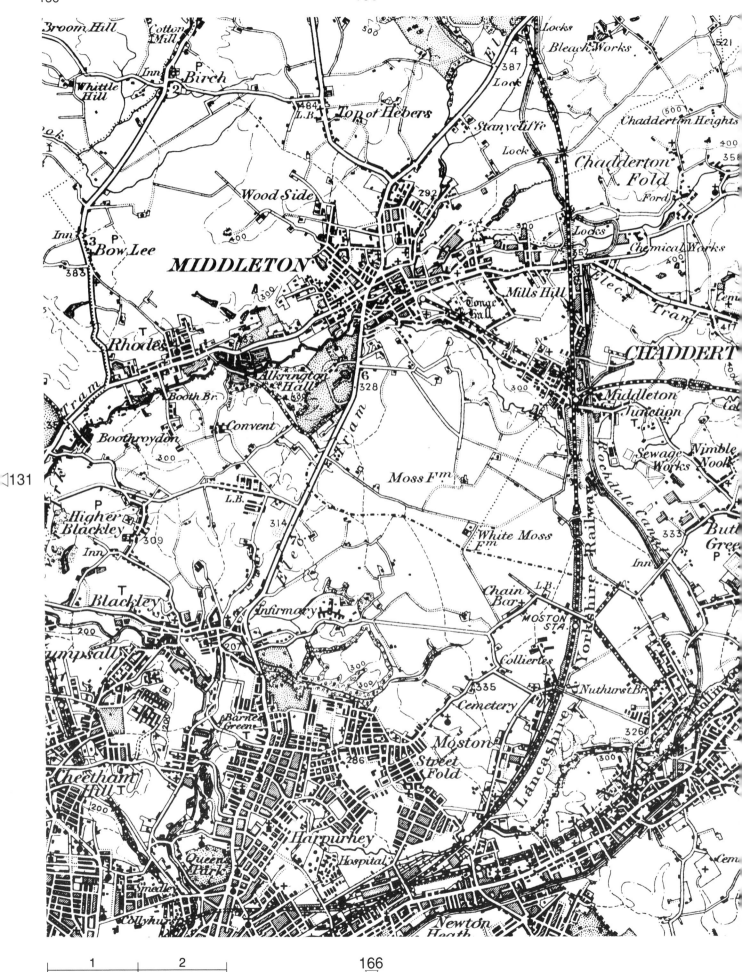

Broom Hill
Cotton Mill
Locks
Bleach Works
521

Whittle Hill
Inn
P
Birch
L.B.
Top of Hebers
Stanycliffe
4
387
Lock
Chadderton Heights
500

Wood Side
292
Lock
300
Chadderton X Fold
400
35
Ford

Inn
3
P
Bow Lee
MIDDLETON
Locks
352
Chemical Works
400

388
300
Tonge Hall
Mills Hill
Elec. Tram
417

Rhodes
T
CHADDERT

Tram
Booth Br.
Alkrington Hall
6
328
300
Middleton Junction
T

Boothroydon
Convent
Sewage Works
Nimble Nook

131
300
Moss Fm
335
But Gree
P

L.B.
White Moss Fm
Inn

Higher Blackley
P
314
309
Inn

Chain Bar
L.B.
MOSTON STA

Blackley
T
Infirmary
335
Collieries
326

200
207
300
300
Nuthurst Br

Barne Green
T
Cemetery

Cheetham Hill
T
286
Moston Street Fold
300

200
Harpurhey

Queen Park
Hospital
Cem

Collyhu
Newton Heath

1   2

1 mile approx.

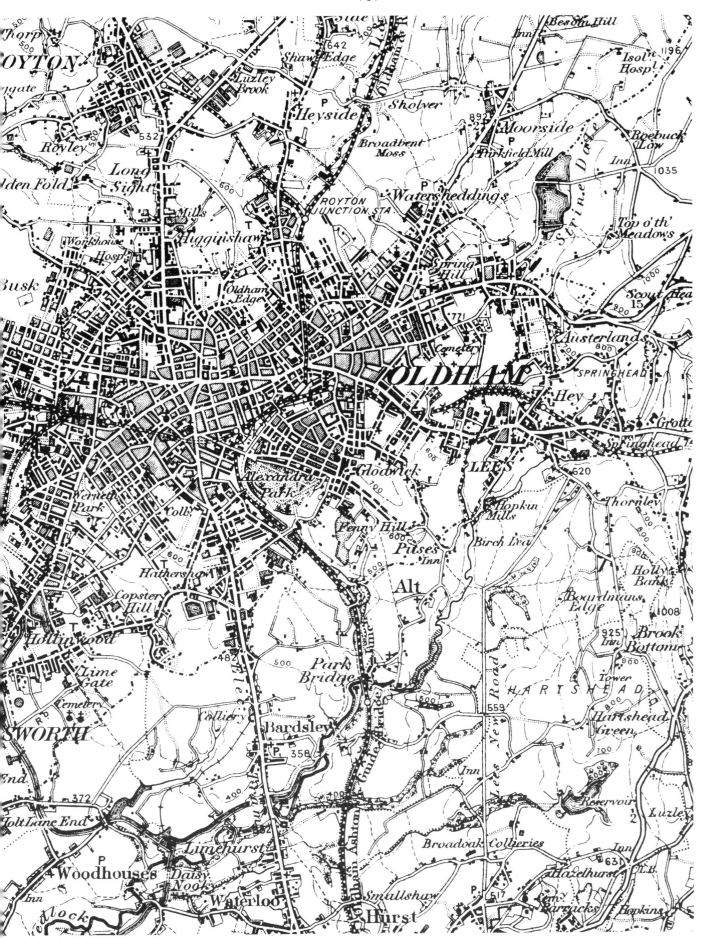

Surveyed 1844 - 47. Revised 1910. Published 1912.

1   2

1 mile approx.

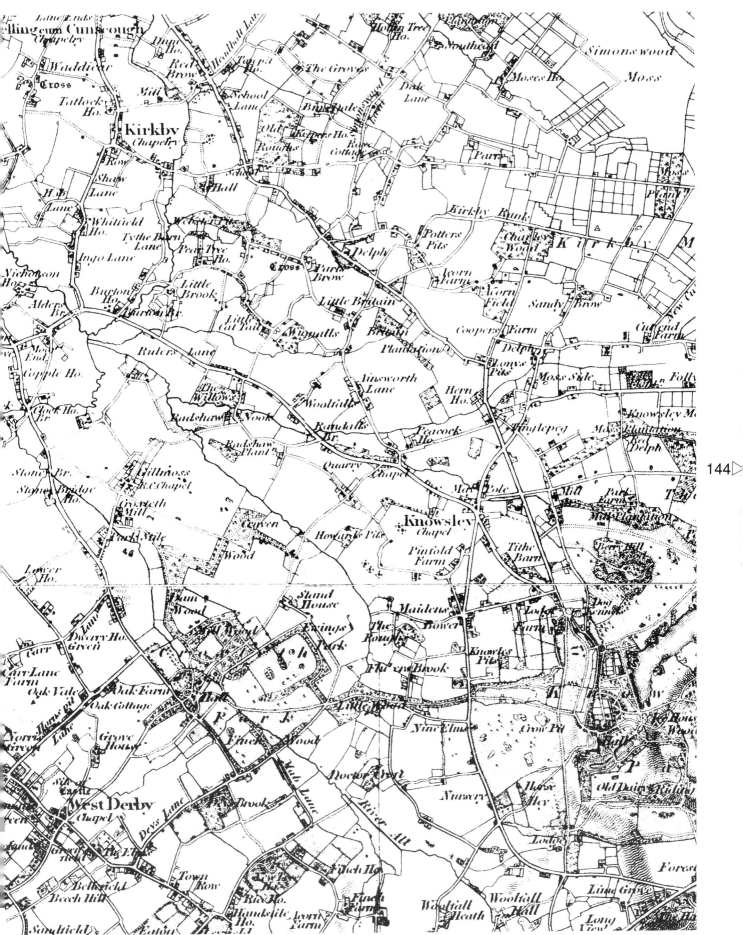

144 ▷

Published 1840 - 1844.

1	2

1 mile approx.

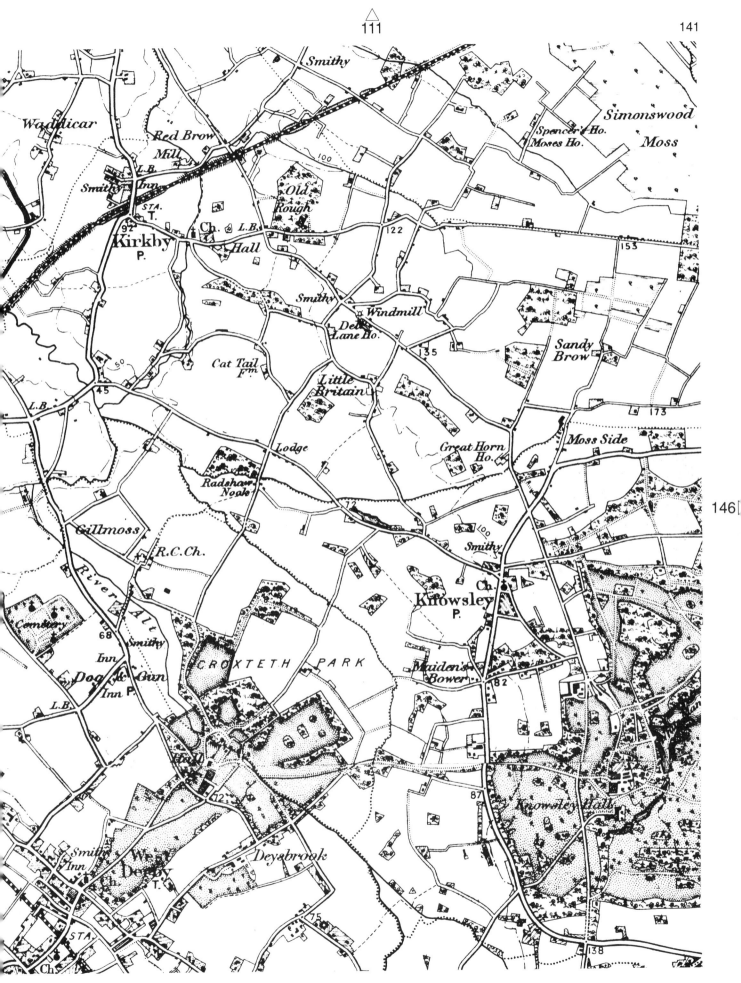

1 mile approx.

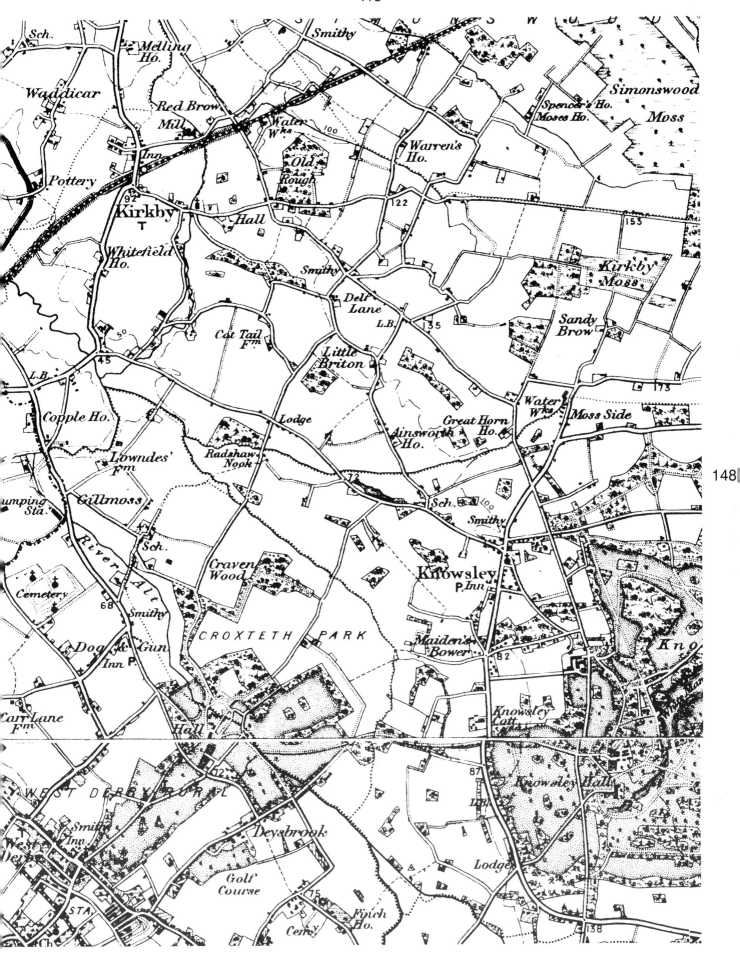

Sch.

Melling
Ho.

Smithy

Simonswood

Waddicar

Red Brow

Spencer's Ho.
Moses Ho.

Moss

Mill

Water
Wks

100

Inn

Warren's
Ho.

Pottery

Old
Rough

122

92

Kirkby
T

Hall

153

Kirkby
Moss

Whitefield
Ho.

Smithy

Delf
Lane

Sandy
Brow

50

L.B.

135

Cot Tail
Fm

Little
Briton

L.B.

173

45

Water
Wks

Moss Side

L.B.

Copple Ho.

Lodge

Great Horn
Ho.

Ainsworth
Ho.

Radshaw
Nook

148

Lowndes'
Fm

72

umping
Sta.

Gillmoss

Sch.

Sch.

100

Smithy

River Alt

Craven
Wood

Knowsley
P. Inn

Cemetery

68

Smithy

CROXTETH   PARK

Dog & Gun
Inn

Maiden's
Bower

82

Kno

Carr Lane
Fm

Knowsley
Cott.

Hall

87

WEST DERBY RURAL

Knowsley Hall

Smithy
Inn

Deysbrook

L.B.

West
Der

Golf
Course

Lodge

STA.

75

Finch
Ho.

Cem.

Ch.

138

Surveyed 1844 - 47 / 1869 - 75. Revised 1904 - 10. Published 1906 - 12.

1   2

1 mile approx.

150

Published 1840 - 1844.

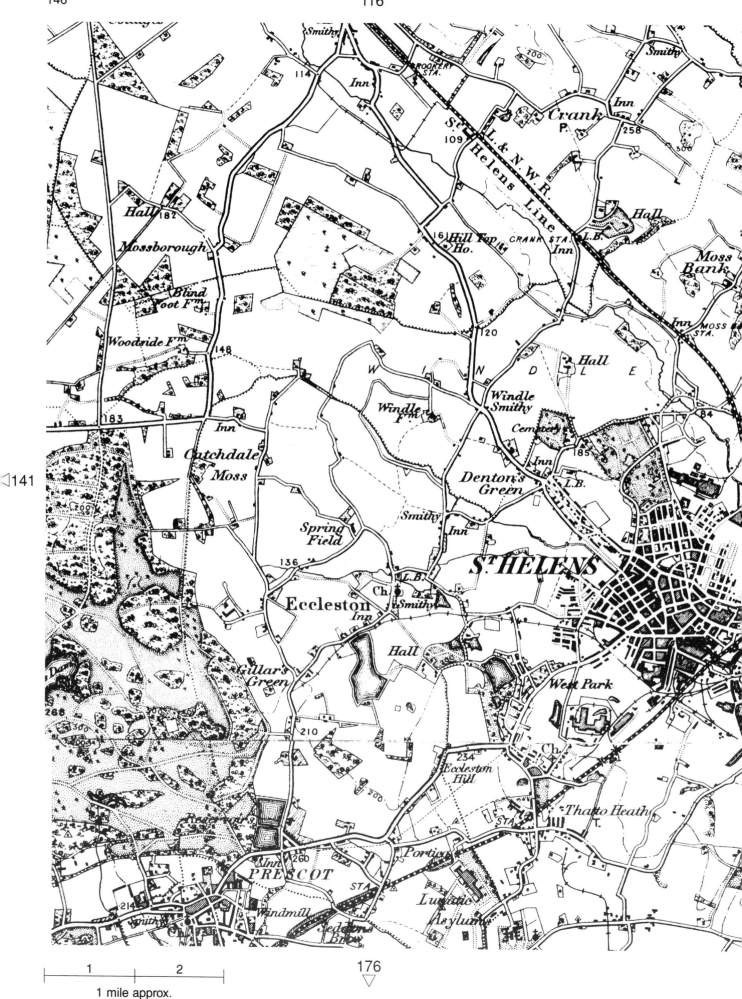

Smithy

114

Inn

Crank
P.

Inn

258

ROOKERY
STA.

St

L. & N. W. R.

St Helens Line

109

161 Hill Top
Ho.

CRANK STA.

Inn

L.B.

Hall

300

Moss
Bank

120

Inn

MOSS
STA.

Hall 182

Mossborough

Blind
Foot Fm

Woodside Fm

148

183

Hall

W   I   N   D   L   E

84

Windle
Fm

Windle
Smithy

185

Inn

Inn

Catchdale
Moss

Cemetery

Denton's
Green

L.B.

200

Smithy

Inn

Spring
Field

136

Smithy

St HELENS

L.B.

Ch.

Smithy

Eccleston
Inn

Gillar's
Green

Hall

West Park

D.

288

300

210

Ch.

Eccleston
Hill

234

Thatto Heath

200

STA.

Reservoir

Portico

Blind 260

PRESCOT

Lunatic
Asylum

STA.

214

Windmill

Smithy

Sedden
Brow

1   2

1 mile approx.

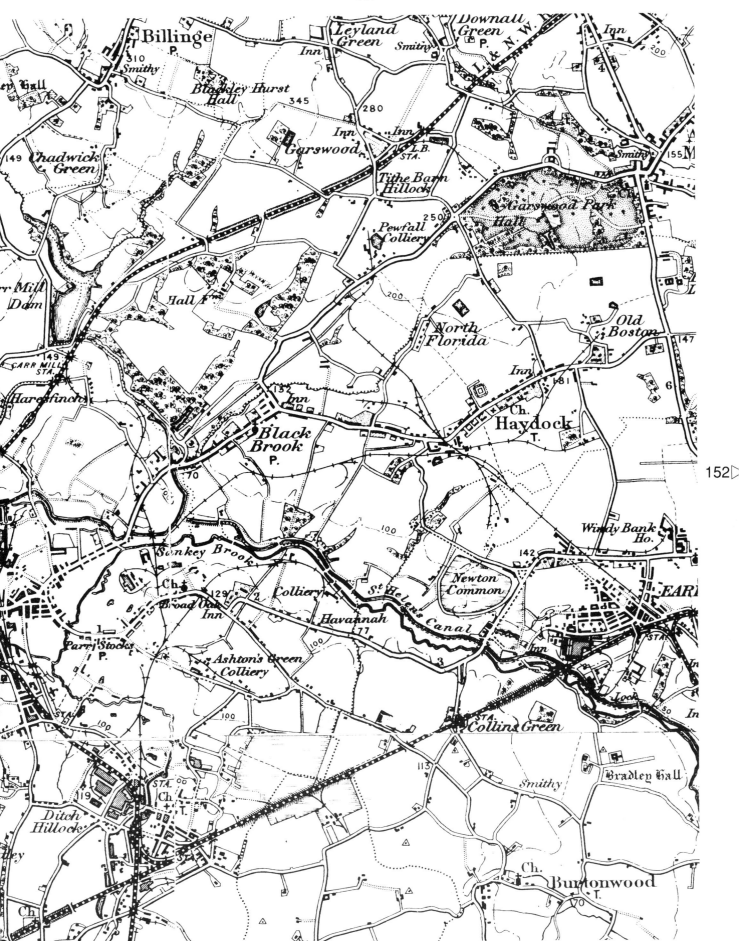

152 ▷

Surveyed 1869 - 74 / 1889 - 92. Revised 1892 - 95. Published 1896.

1   2

1 mile approx.

Billinge

Leyland
Green

Downall
Green

L. & N. W.

Inn

Smithy

310

Blackley Hurst
Hall

Aqueduct

345

280

Inn

200

Chadwick
Green

Garswood
P.

Rivington to Liverpool W. Wks.

Tithe Barn
Hillock

155

Colt

149

WINSTANLEY
DET.

BILLINGE
CHAPEL END
(DET.)

250

Garswood Park

Hall

4

Pewfall
Colliery

Old Garswood
Hall F.

200

North
Florida

St. Helens Br.

Old
Boston

14

rr Mill
Dam

149

New
Boston

Elec. Tram

6

CARR MILL
STA.

132

G.C.

Haresfinch

181

Haydock
T.

Black
Brook
P.

154 ▷

70

Windy Bank
Ho.

Sankey Brook

100

ard's
dge

Broad Oak

129

Colliery

St. Helens Canal

Newton
Common

130

EAR

Havannah

75

Parr
Stocks
T.

Colliery

Derbyshire
Hill

100

Vitriol
Square

Lock

50

190

Smy.

Parr Moss

COLLINS
GREEN STA.

113

Collins
Green
T.

Bradley Hall

Loc

Hosp!

119

Makin's
Row

Smithy

Ch.

Ditch
Hillock

Inn

R.C.

Bold
Colliery

L.B.

Burtonwood
T.

Iron
Works

Inn

Cem!

70

Surveyed 1844 - 47 / 1869 - 75. Revised 1904 - 10. Published 1906 - 12.

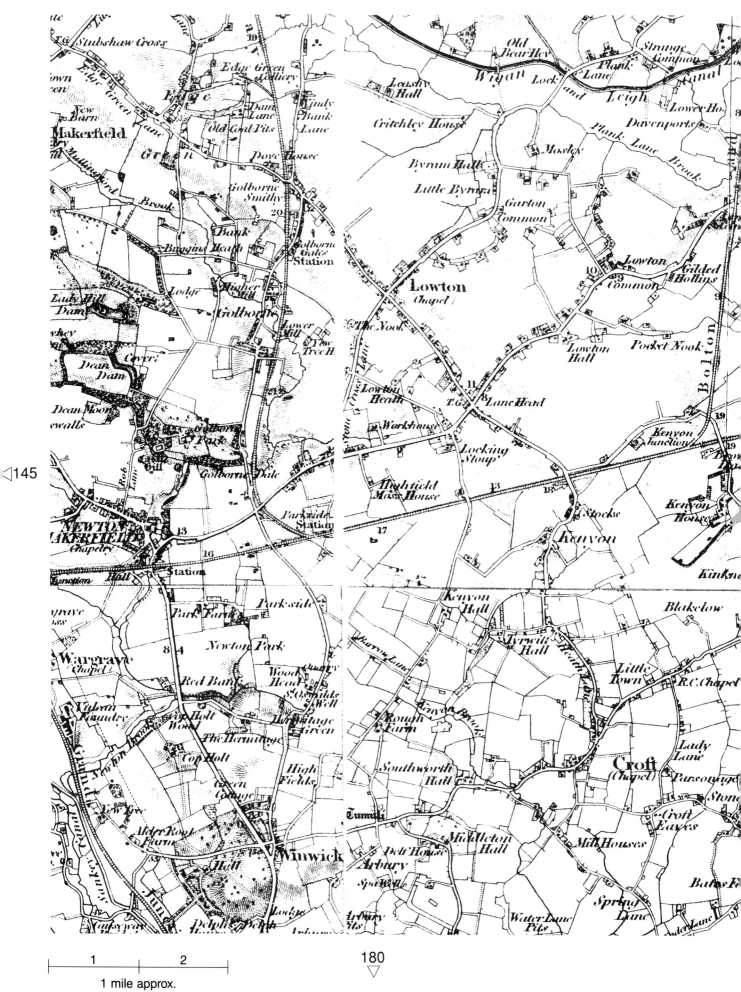

1 mile approx.

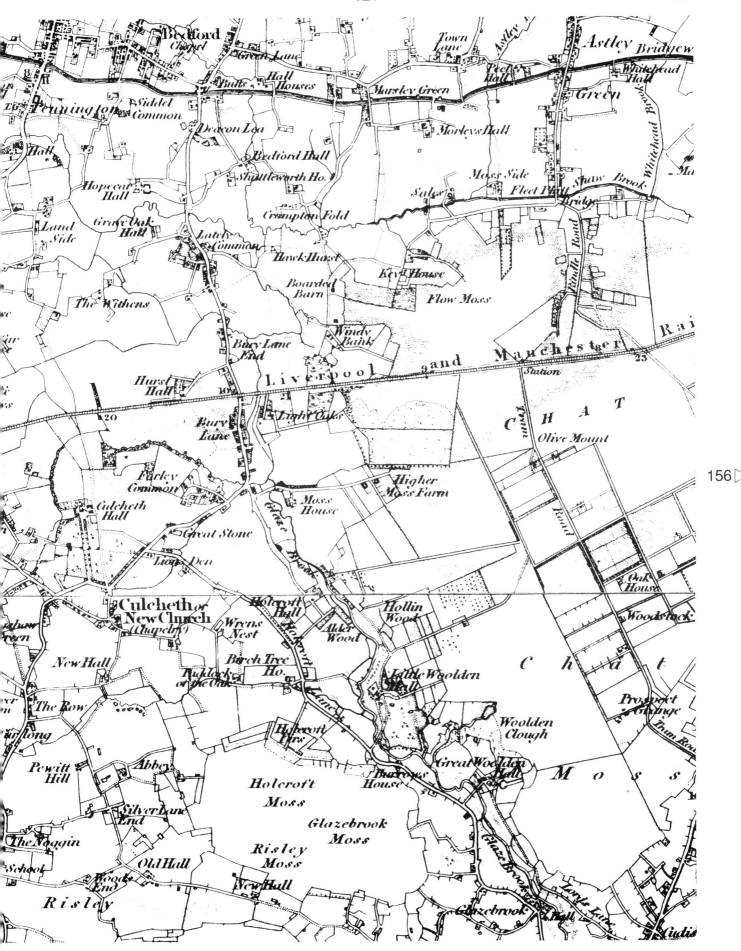

Bedford
Church
Great Lane
Town
Lane
Astley
Astley Bridge w
Pennington
Siddel
Common
Butts
Hall
Houses
Marsley Green
Peel
Hall
Green
Whitehead
Hall
Deacon Lea
Morleys Hall
Whitehead Brook
Hall
Bedford Hall
Hopecarr
Hall
Shuttleworth Ho.
Moss Side
Salem
Fleet Field
Shaw Brook
Ma
Land
Side
Grace Oak
Hall
Crampton Fold
Bridge
Bridle Road
Lately
Common
Hawk Hurst
Keys House
Flow Moss
Ra
The Withens
Boarded
Barn
23
Bury Lane
End
Windy
Bank
Liverpool
and
Manchester
Station
Olive Mount
C H A T
Hurst
Hall
10
20
Bury
Lane
21
Light Oaks
Farley
Common
Moss
House
Higher
Moss Farm
Road
Culcheth
Hall
Great Stone
Glaze Brook
Oak
House
Lions Den
Culcheth or
New Church
(Chapelry)
Holcroft
Hall
Hollin
Wood
Woodstock
Wrens
Nest
Alder
Wood
C h a t
New Hall
Birch Tree
Ho.
Little Woolden
Hall
Paddock
of the Oak
Holcroft Lane
The Row
Holcroft
Firs
Woolden
Clough
Prospect
Grange
Thum Road
Pewitt
Hill
Abbey
Burrows
House
Great Woolden
Hall
M o s s
Holcroft
Moss
Silver Lane
End
Glazebrook
Moss
The Noggin
Risley
Moss
Glazebrook
School
Old Hall
Woods
End
New Hall
R i s l e y
Glazebrook Hall
Little Lane
udis

Published 1840 - 1844.

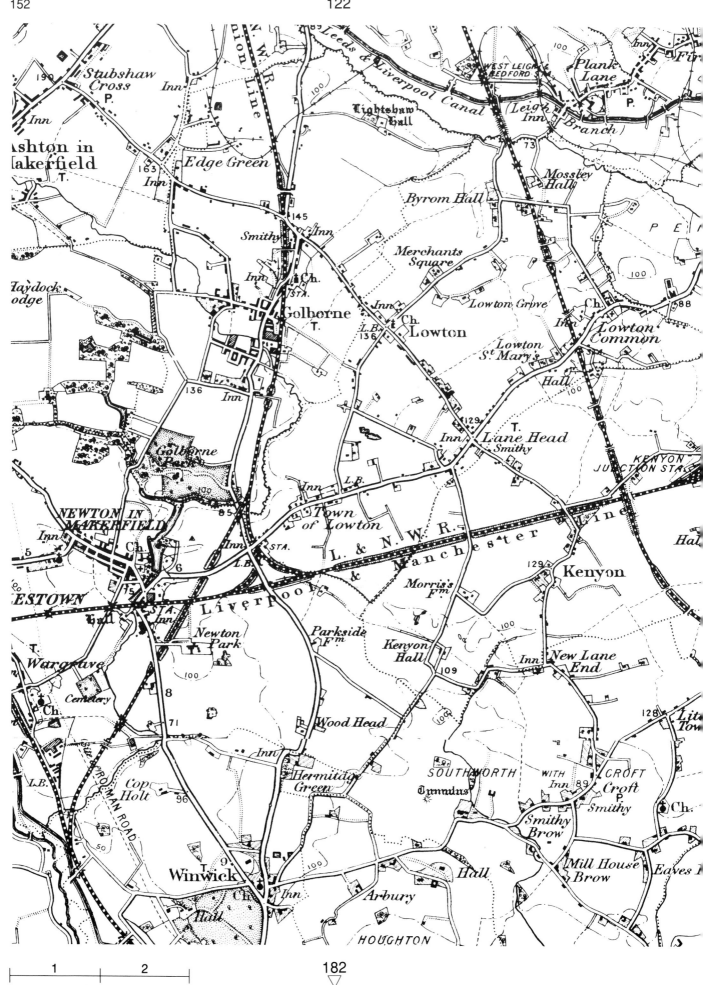

Stubshaw
Cross
P.

Inn

Inn

Ashton in
Makerfield
T.

163

Edge Green

Inn

Haydock
Lodge

Smithy

Inn

Ch.
STA.

Golborne
T.

136

Inn

Golborne
Park

100

NEWTON IN
MAKERFIELD

Inn

Ch.
6

5

85

STA.
Inn

L.B.

ESTOWN

Hall

STA.
Inn

Wargrave

T.

Newton
Park

Cemetery

Ch.

8

71

100

L.B.

Cop
Holt

96

ROMAN ROAD

50

Winnick
T.

Hall

Ch.

Inn

Leeds & Liverpool Canal

WEST LEIGH &
BEDFORD STA.

Plank
Lane
P.

100

Inn

Lightshaw
Hall

Leigh
Inn

(Branch)

73

Byrom Hall

Mossley
Hall

P E

Merchants
Square

Lowton Grove

Inn

Ch.
Lowton

Lowton
Common

Ch.

STA.

88

L.B.
136

Lowton
St Mary's

Hall

Hall

100

129

T.

Inn

Lane Head
Smithy

KENYON
JUNCTION STA.

Inn

L.B.

Town
of Lowton

L & N.W.R.

Manchester

129

Kenyon

Morris's
Fm.

Hall

Parkside
Fm.

Kenyon
Hall

109

Inn

New Lane
End

128

Lit
Tow

Wood Head

SOUTHWORTH

WITH
Inn

CROFT

Croft
P.

Smithy

Ch.

Inn

Hermitage
Green

Terminus

4

89

Smithy
Brow

Mill House
Brow

Eaves

9

Hall

100

Inn

Arbury

HOUGHTON

1		2

1 mile approx.

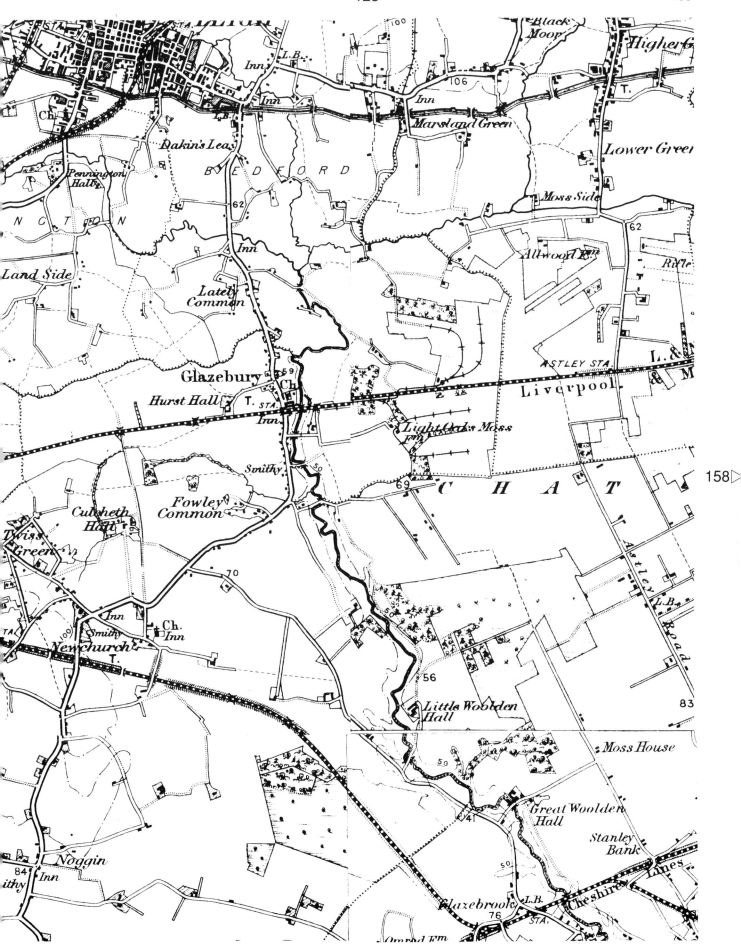

Surveyed 1869 - 75. Revised 1892 - 95. Published 1896.

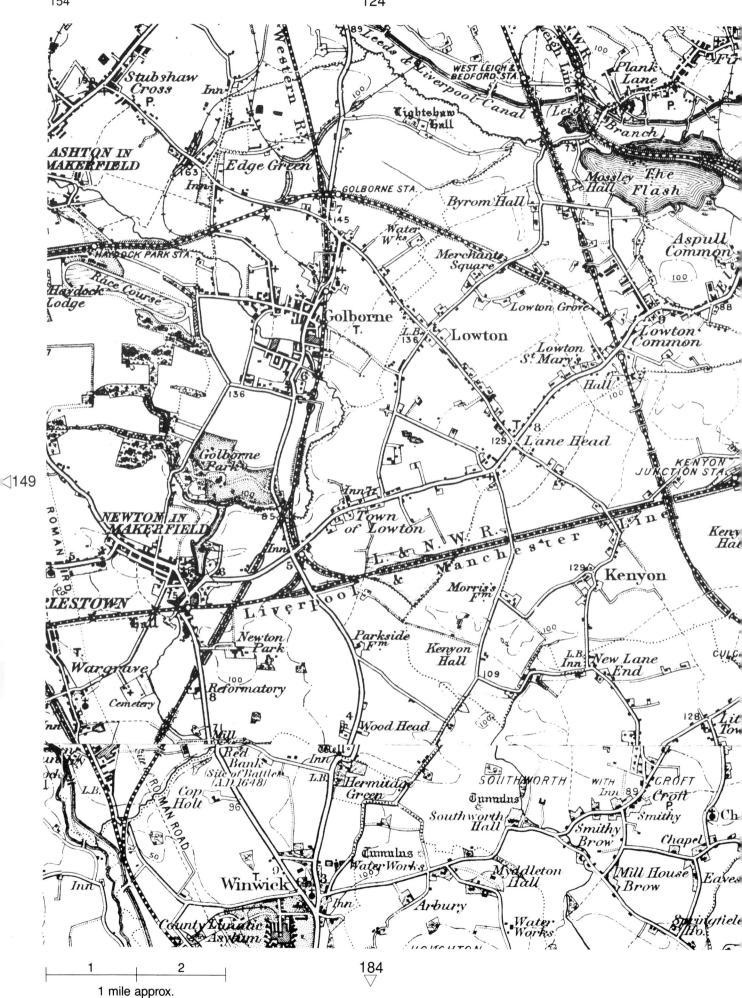

149

1 mile approx.

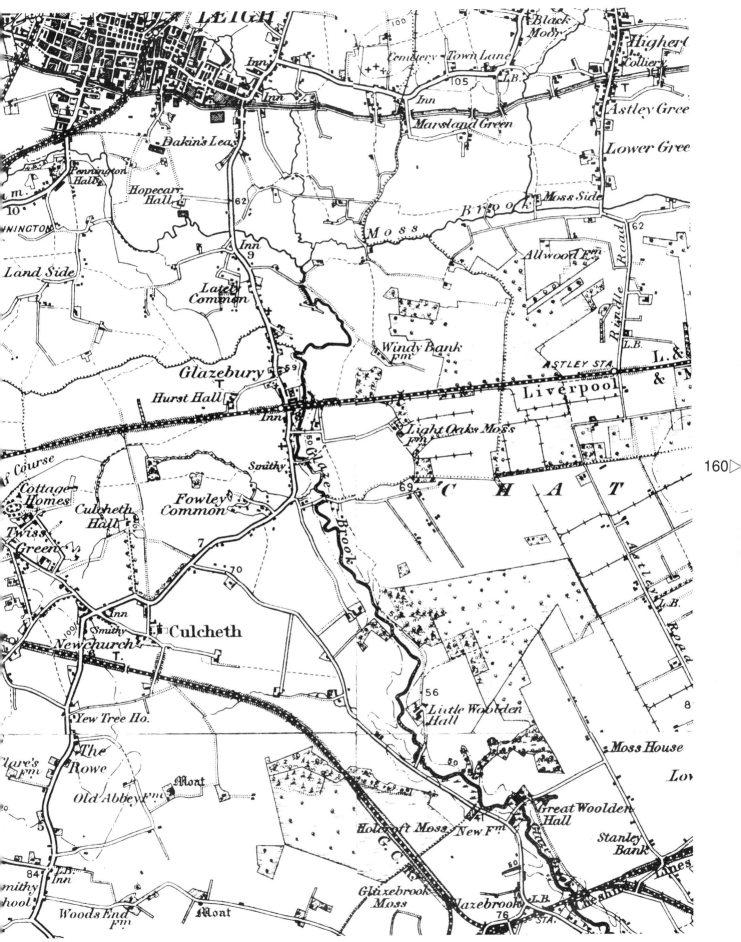

Surveyed 1844 - 47 / 1870 - 75. Revised 1904 - 10. Published 1906 - 12.

1   2

1 mile approx.

162 ▷

Published 1840 - 1844.

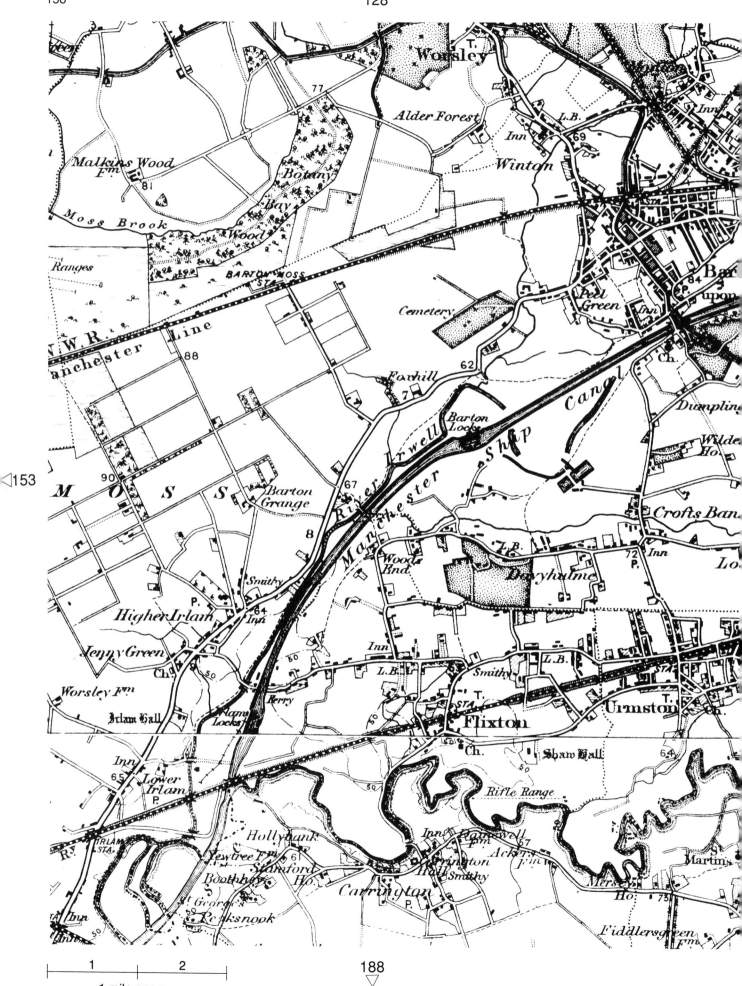

◁153

1 mile approx.

164▷

Surveyed 1870 - 75. Revised 1895. Published 1896.

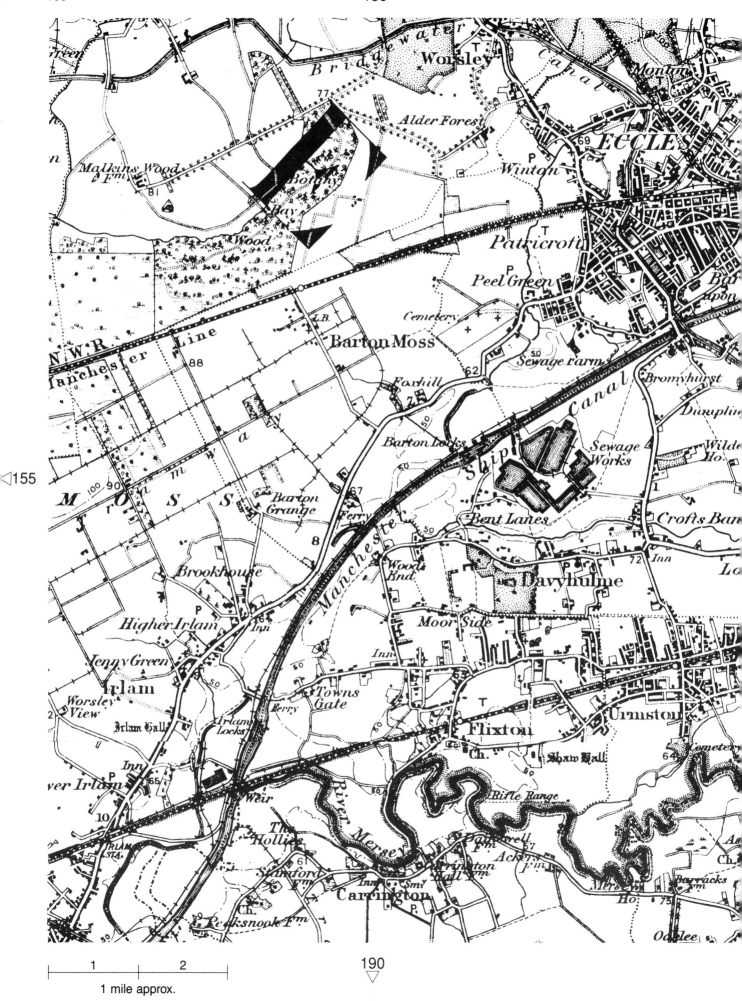

155

190

1

2

1 mile approx.

166▷

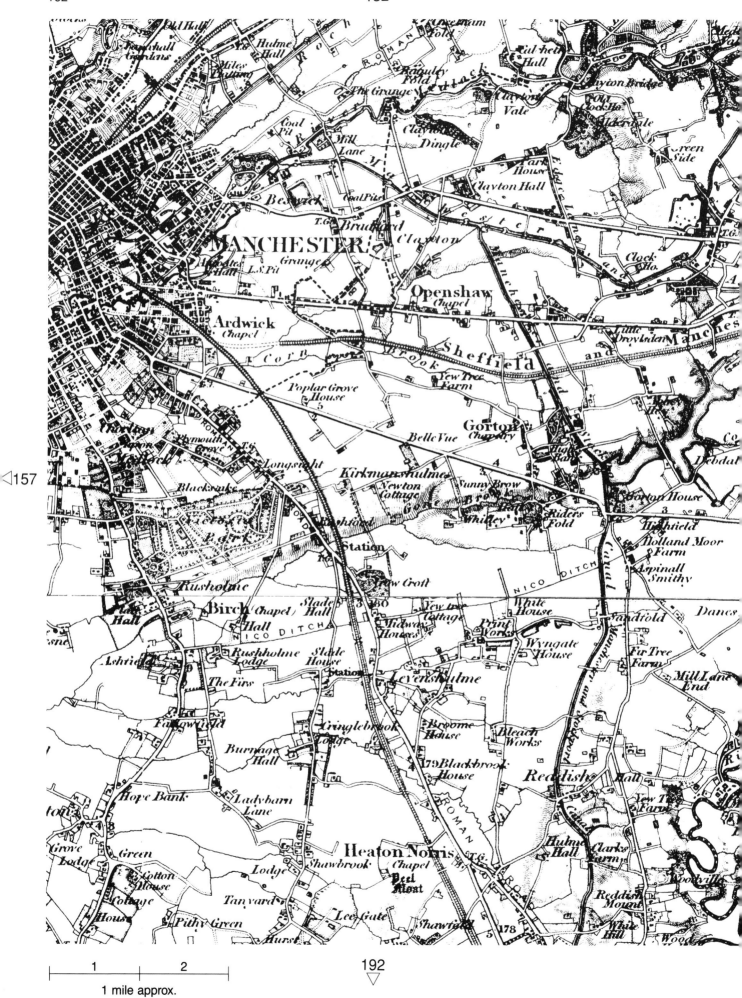

1 mile approx.

Published 1840 - 1844.

1   2

1 mile approx.

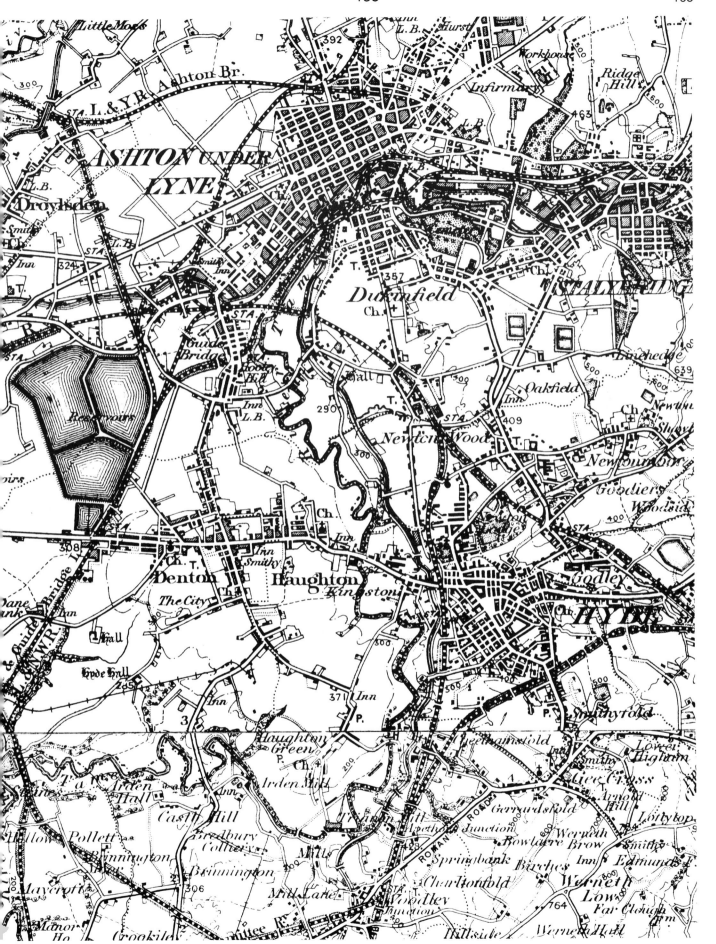

Surveyed 1870 - 75. Revised 1895. Published 1896.

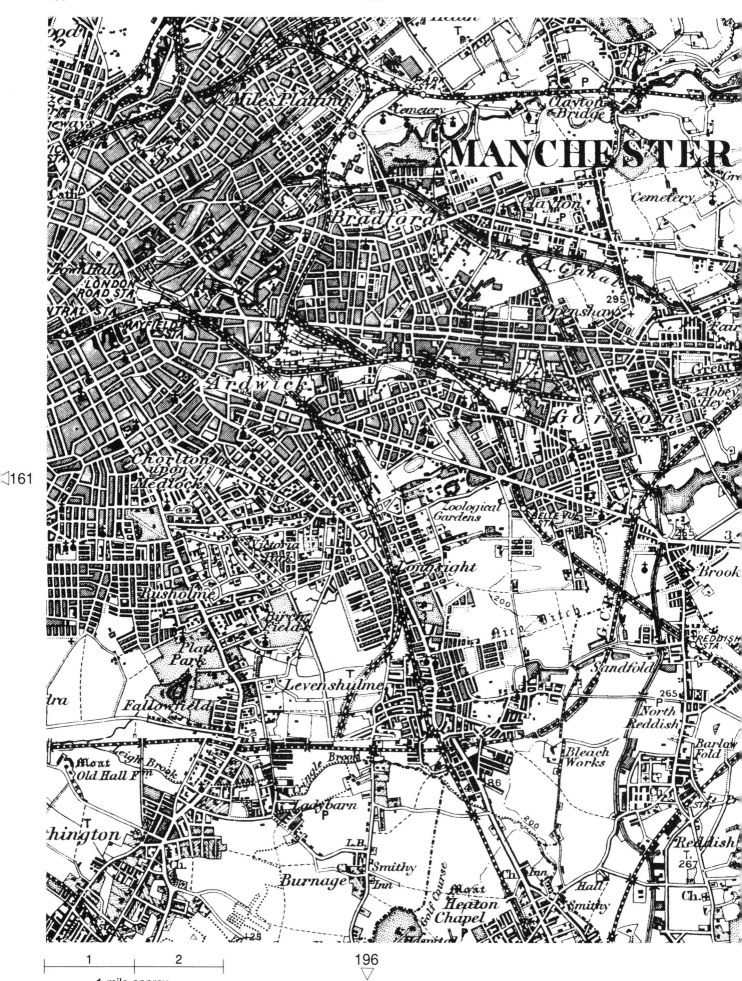

1 mile approx.

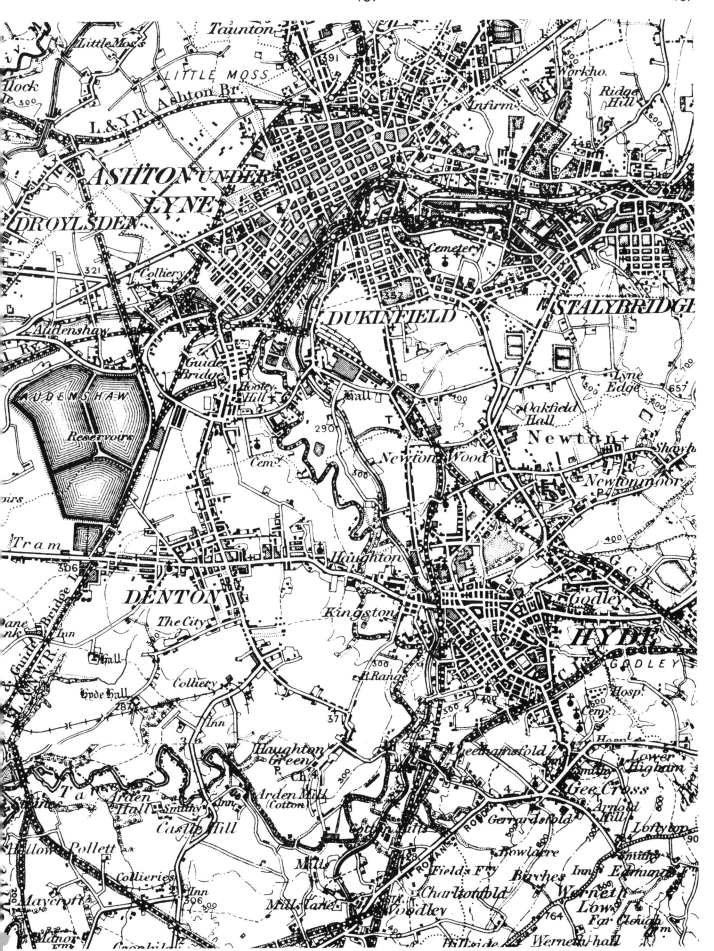

Surveyed 1844 - 47 / 1870 - 75. Revised 1904 - 10. Published 1906 - 12.

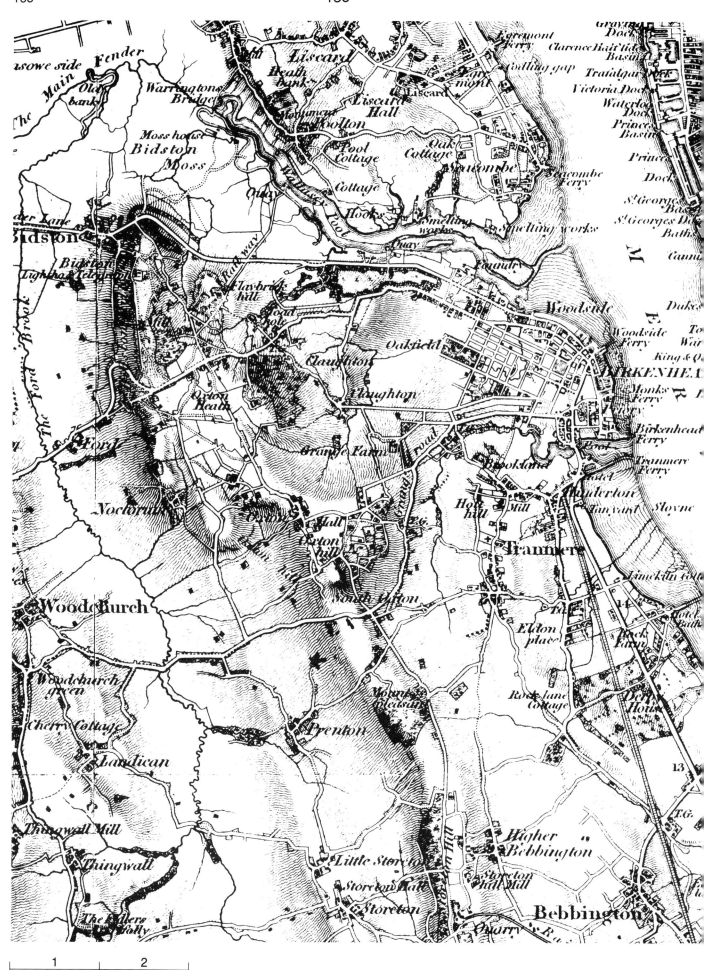

1 mile approx.

174▷

Published 1840 - 1844.

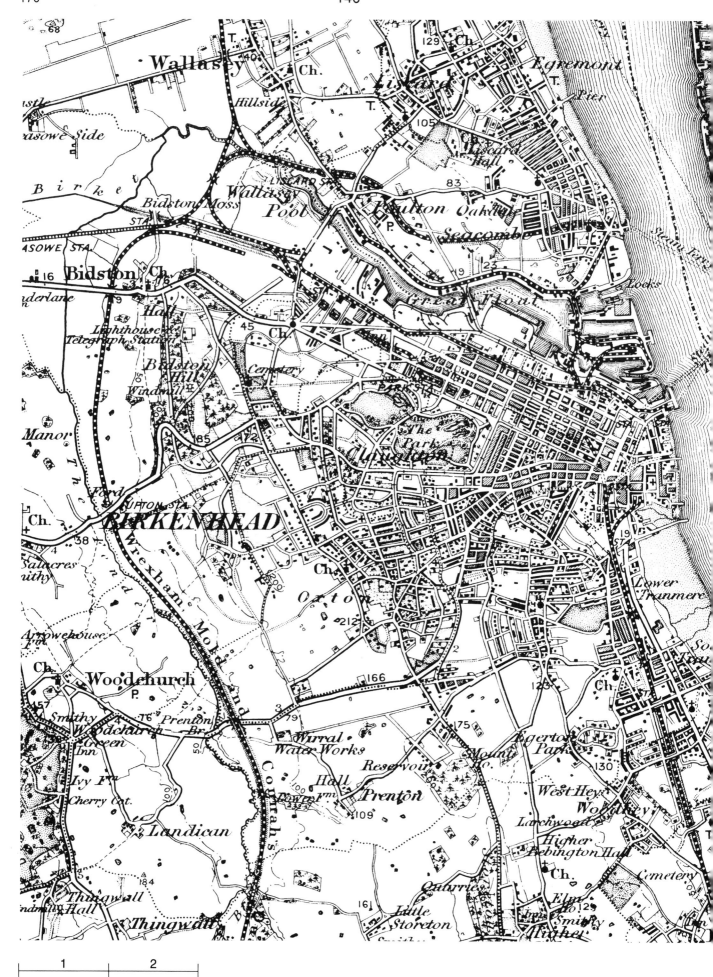

Wallasey

Hillside

asowe Side

Birke

Bidston Moss

Wallasey Pool

Liscard

Egremont

Pier

Liscard Hall

Poulton

Oakdale

Seacombe

asowe STA.

Bidston Ch.

derlane

Hall

Lighthouse & Telegraph Station

Bidston Hill

Windmill

Cemetery

Ch.

Great Float

Locks

Manor

The

Ford

SUTTON STA.

BIRKENHEAD

Ch.

The Park

Claughton

Salacres mithy

Wrexham, Mold and

Oxton

Lower Tranmere

Arrowehouse

Ch.

Woodchurch
P.

Smithy

Woodchurch Green

Inn

Prenton Br.

Wirral Water Works

Reservoir

Egerton Park

Ivy F.m

Mount

West Hey

Larchwood

Cherry Cot.

Hall

Prenton

Landican

Higher Bebington Hall

Ch.

Cemetery

Thingwall Hall

Little Storeton

Elm

Smithy

Higher

Thingwall

RIVER

Everton

College

Edge Hill

Wird

Fairfield
T.

T.

Wavertree

Ch.

Wavertree
Nook

Old Swan
Ch.
T.

L.B.

Smith

T.

Ch.

Toxteth Park

Sefton
Park

Mossley
Hill

Inn

ST.

Inn
ST.

176

RIVER MERSEY

Dingle Pt.

Ferry

Pier

se-hill

Woodhead
Fm

Ch.

Aigburth
T.

STA.

STA.

Grasse
Ch.

STA.

Edge Hill & Garston

STA.

Surveyed 1869 - 74. Revised 1895. Published 1896.

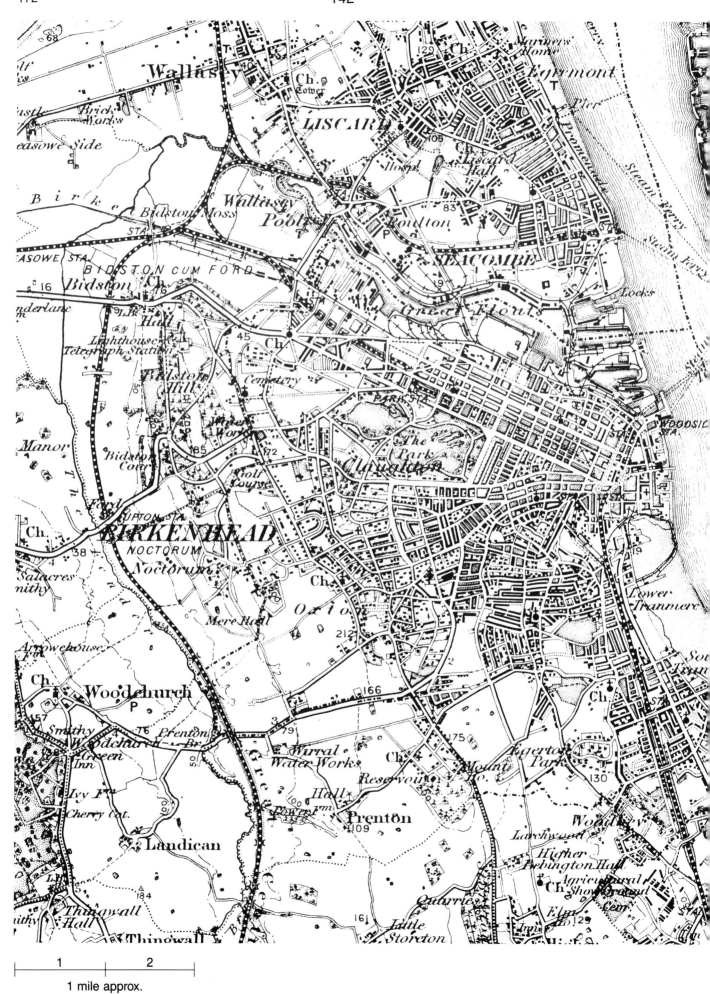

1 mile approx.

178

Surveyed 1869 - 74. Revised 1904. Published 1906.

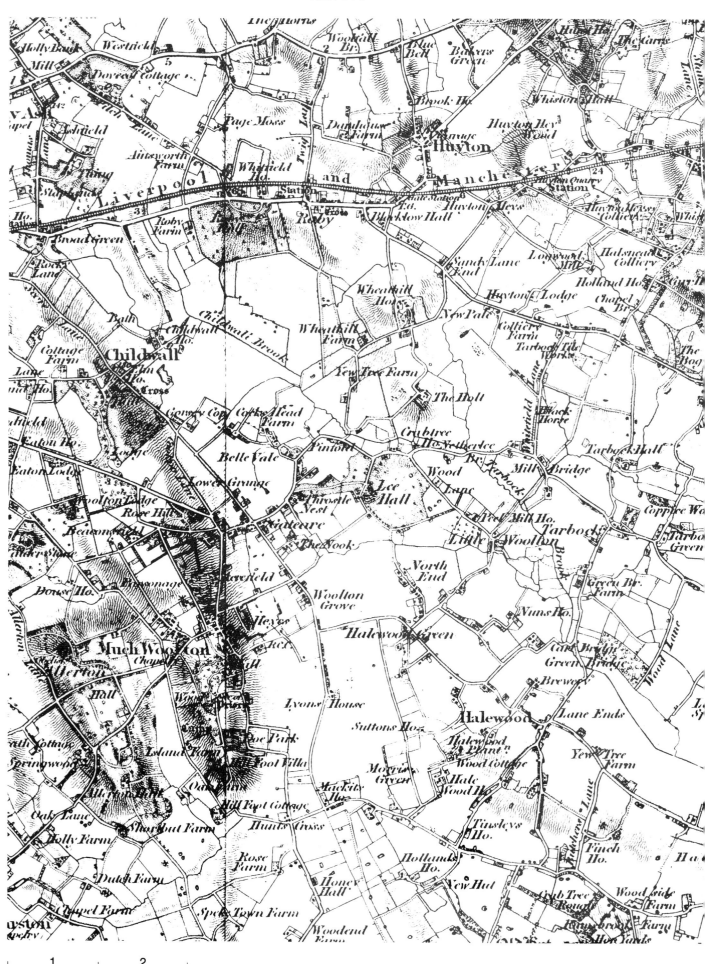

1   2

1 mile approx.

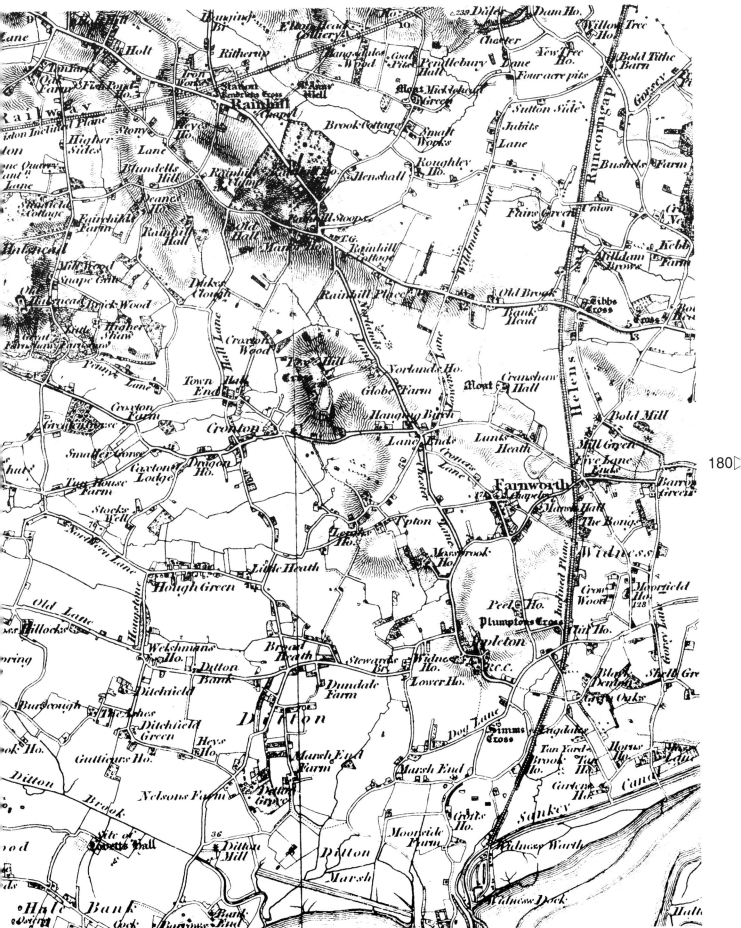

Published 1840 - 1844.

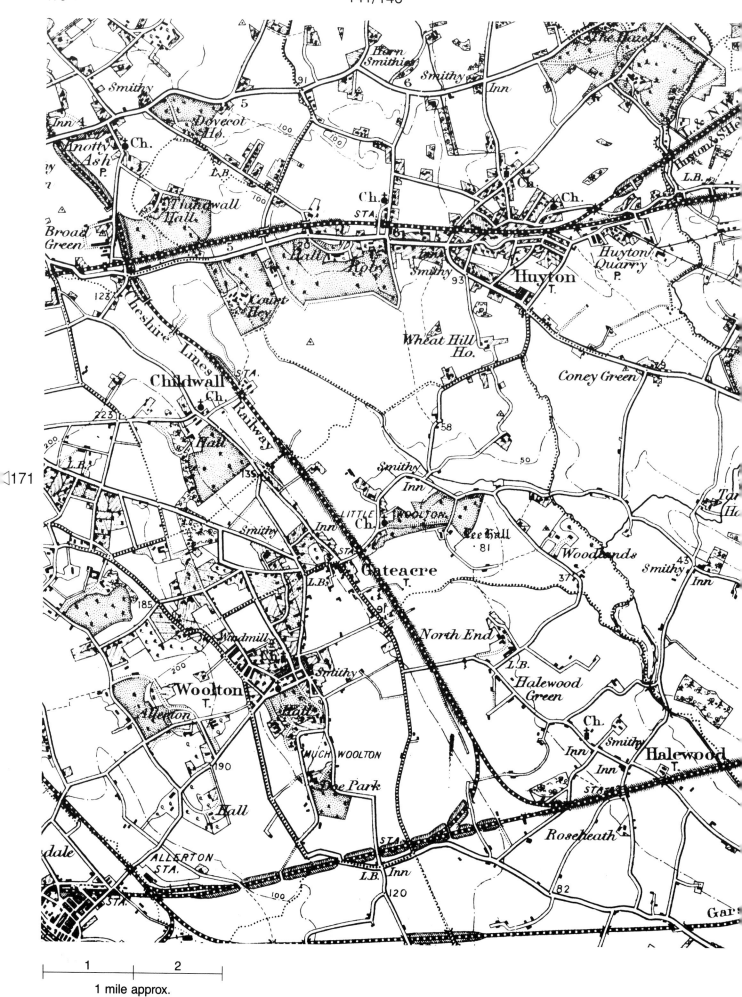

171

1 mile approx.

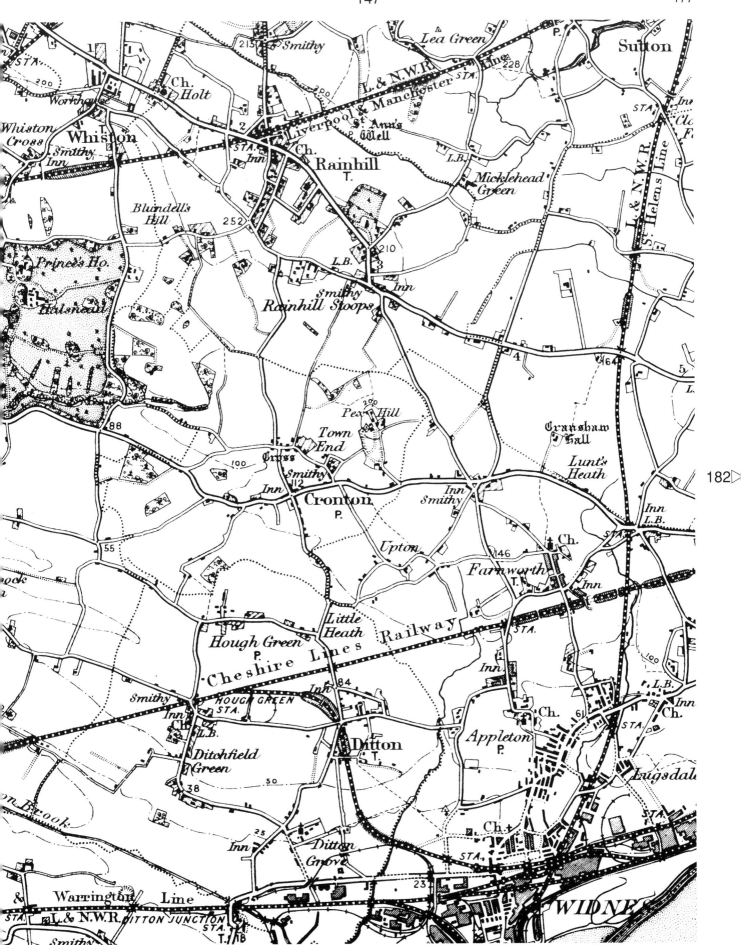

Surveyed 1872 - 75. Revised 1895. Published 1896.

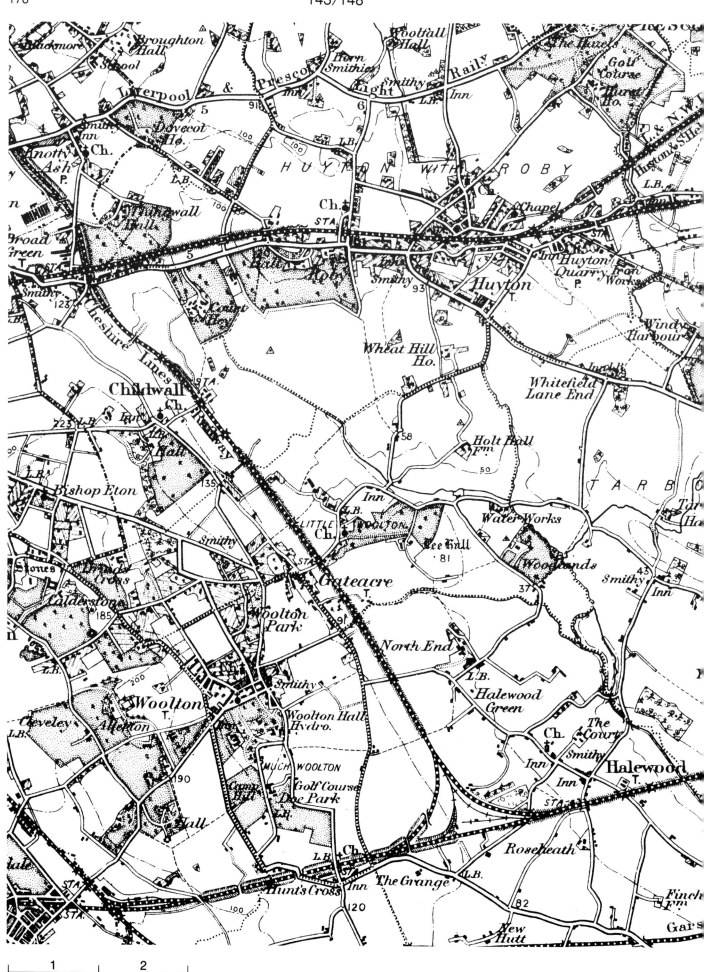

1 mile approx.

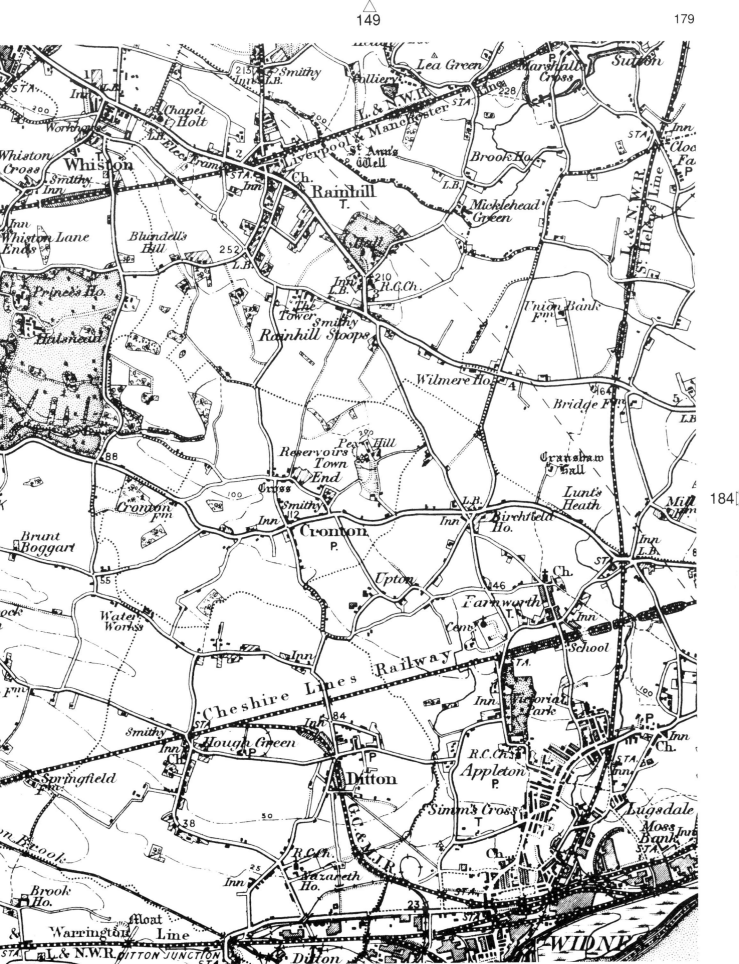

Surveyed 1872 - 75. Revised 1904 - 5. Published 1907.

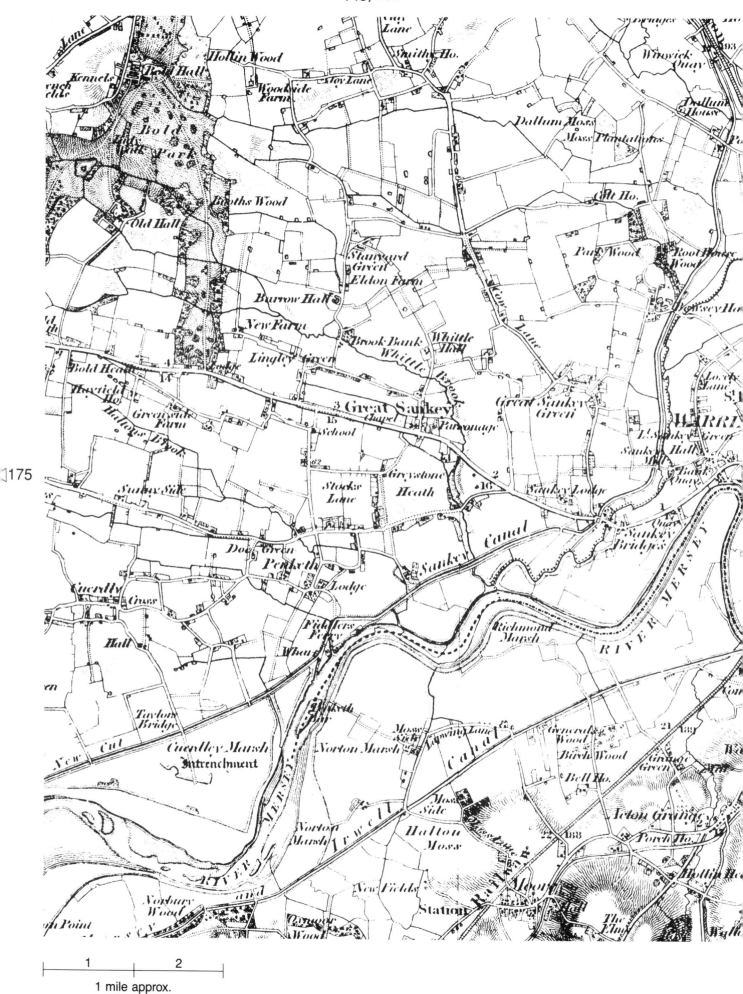

1   2

1 mile approx.

Published 1840 - 1844.

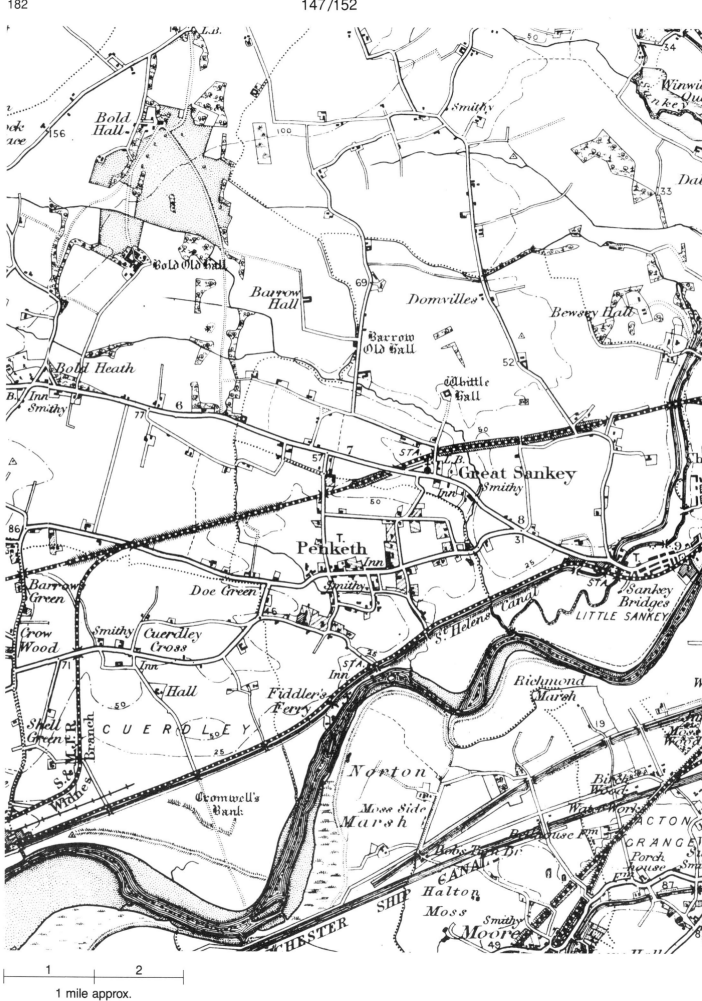

1 mile approx.

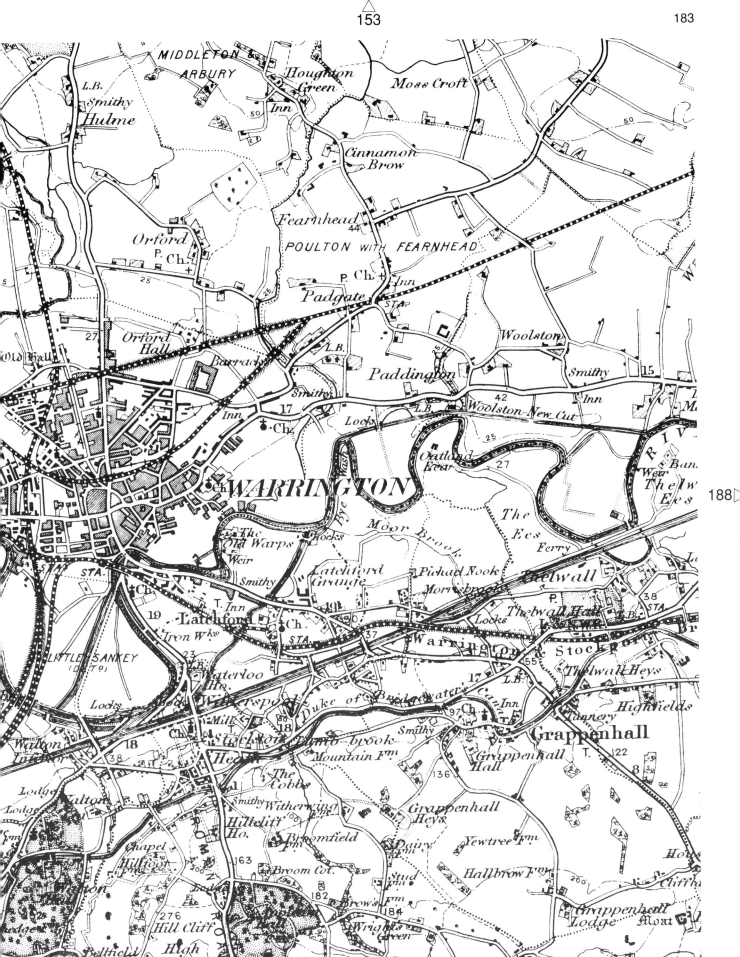

Surveyed 1872 - 75. Revised 1895. Published 1896.

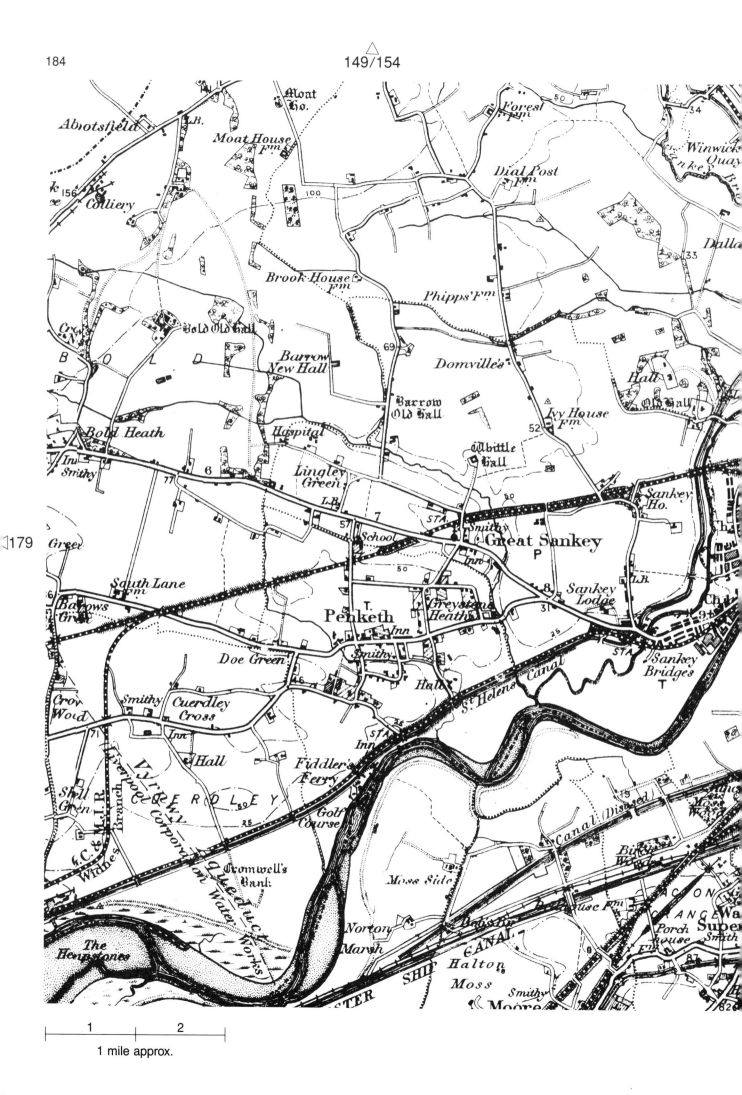

Abbotsfield

Moat Ho.

Forest Fm

Winwick Quay

Moat House Fm

Dial Post Fm

Colliery

156

100

Dalla

Brook House Fm

Phipps' Fm

33

Crow Wood

Bold Old Hall

Domville's

Hall

Barrow New Hall

69

52

Barrow Old Hall

Ivy House Fm

Old Hall

Bold Heath

Hospital

Whittle Hall

Inn

Smithy

Lingley Green

50

Sankey Ho.

179

Green

6

77

L.B.

STA.

57

7

School

Smithy

Great Sankey

P

South Lane Fm

50

Inn

8

L.B.

Barrows Green

Penketh

Greystone Heath

Sankey Lodge

3

Ch

9

Doe Green

Inn

25

STA.

Sankey Bridges

Smithy

Smithy

Hall

St Helens Canal

Crow Wood

Cuerdley Cross

Inn

Hall

Fiddler's Ferry

STA.

Inn

Canal (Disused)

Shell Green

WIDNES

71

WIRREW

Golf Course

50

Moss Side

Birch Wood

House Fm

Cromwell's Bank

25

Norton Marsh

ORANGE

Porch House

Super

L.C. & M.R.

Widnes Branch

Liverpool Corporation Water Works

Babs

Smith

The Hempstones

Halton Moss

Smithy

87

CANAL

MANCHESTER SHIP CANAL

Moore

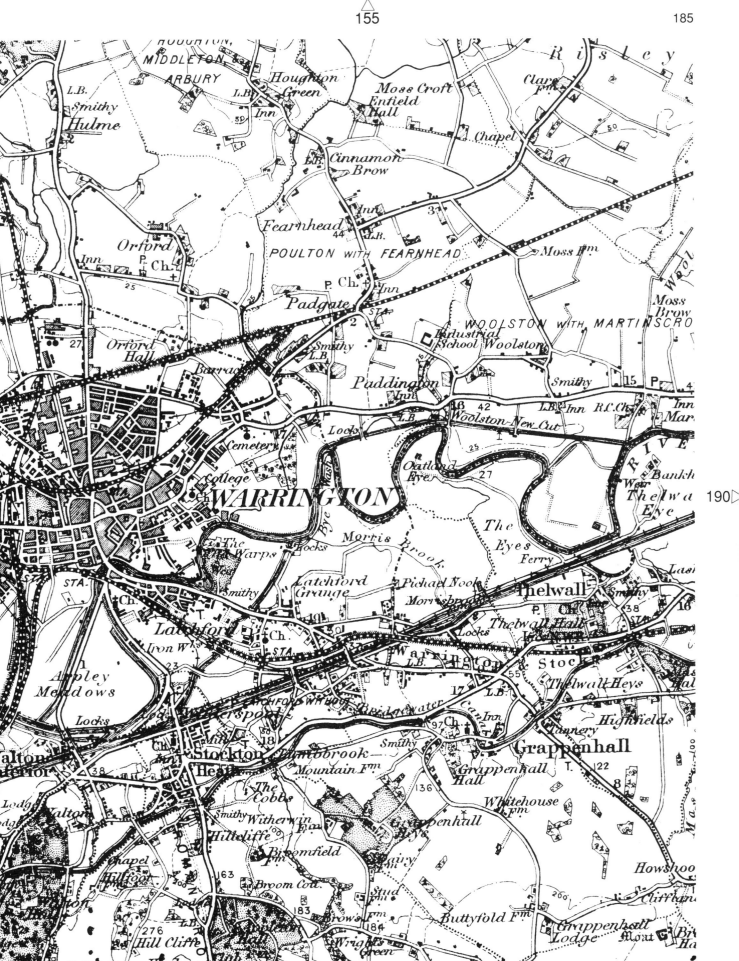

190 ▷

Surveyed 1872 - 75. Revised 1904 - 5. Published 1907.

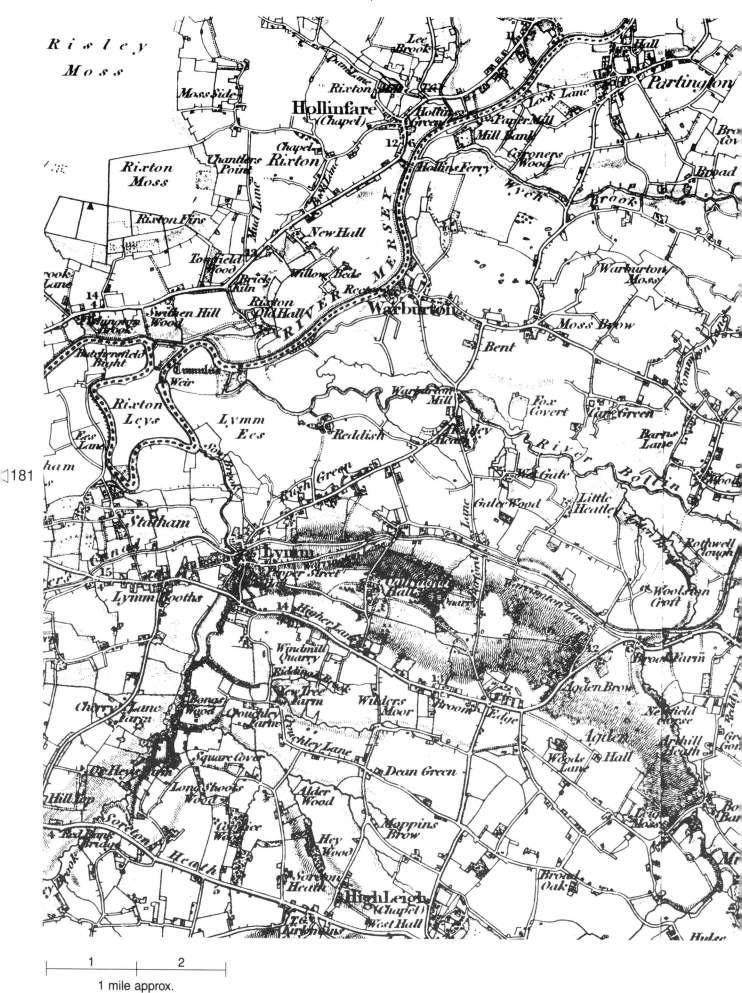

1 mile approx.

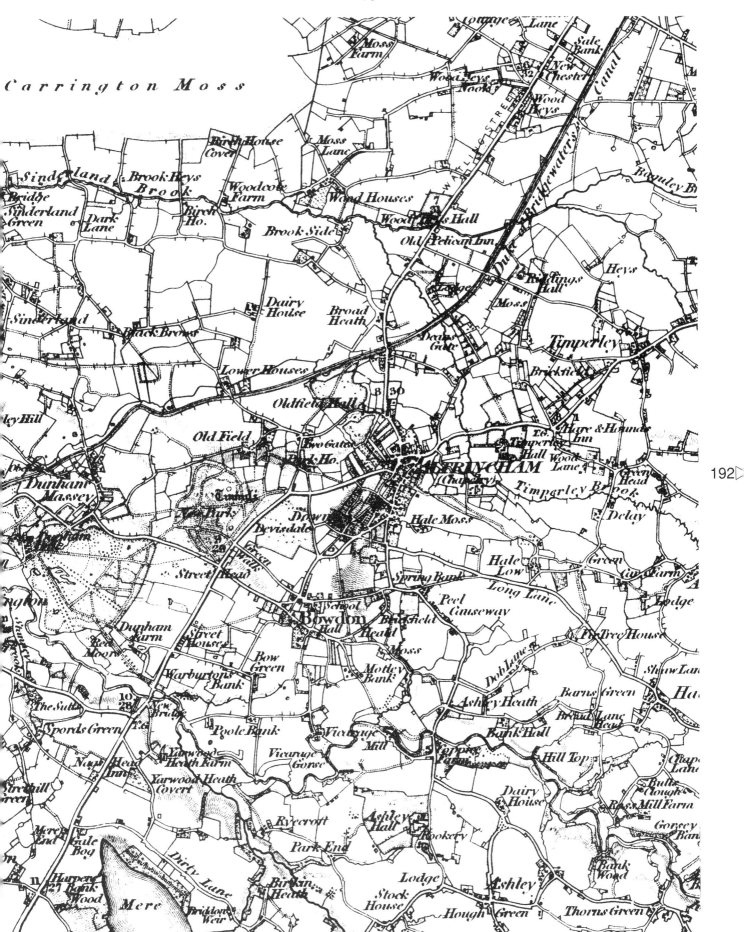

192 ▷

Published 1840 - 1844.

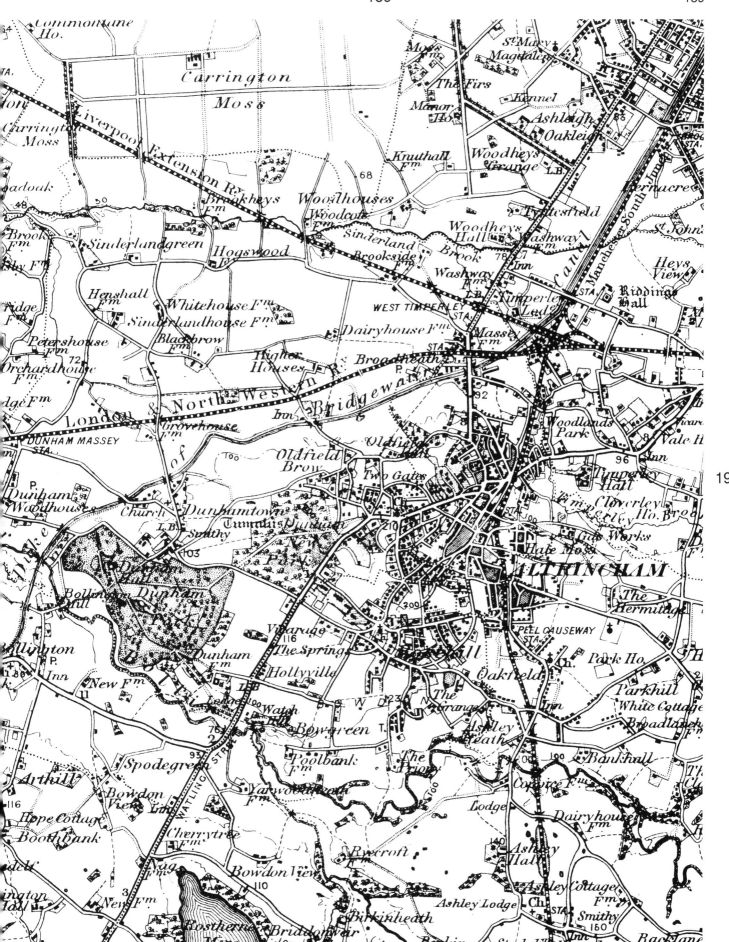

Surveyed 1870 - 75. Revised 1895. Published 1896.

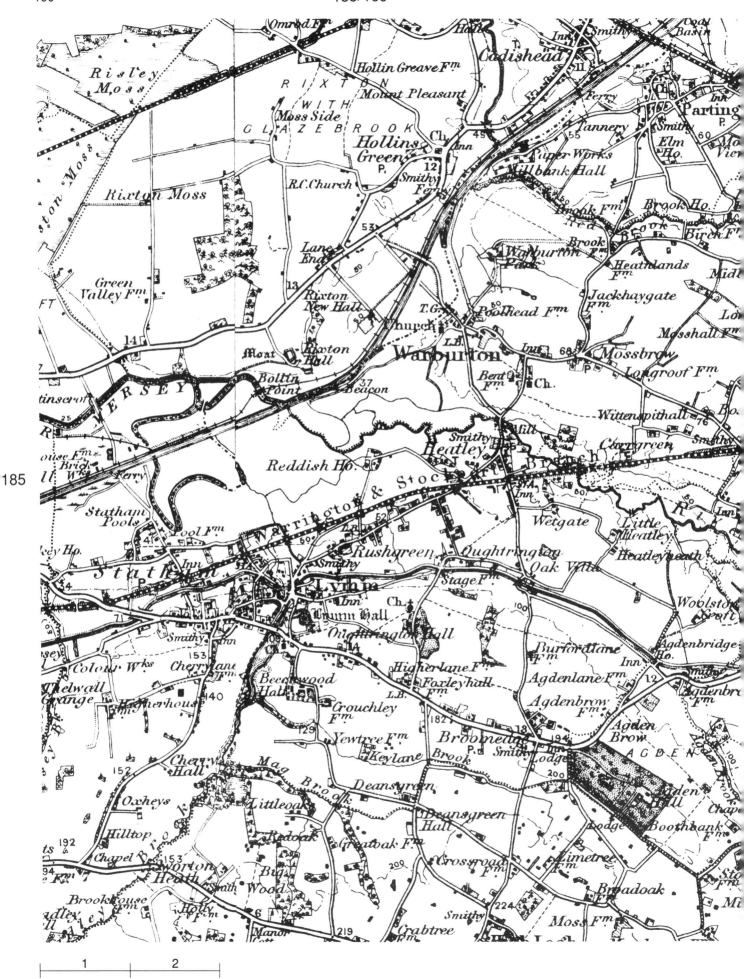

1   2

1 mile approx.

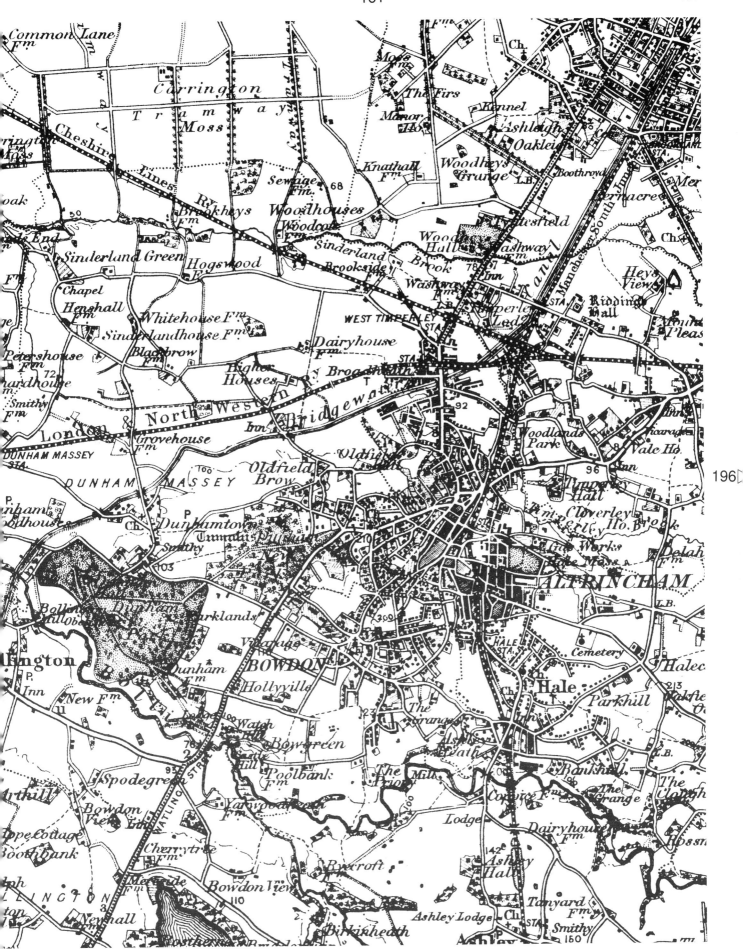

Surveyed 1870 - 75. Revised 1903. Published 1908.

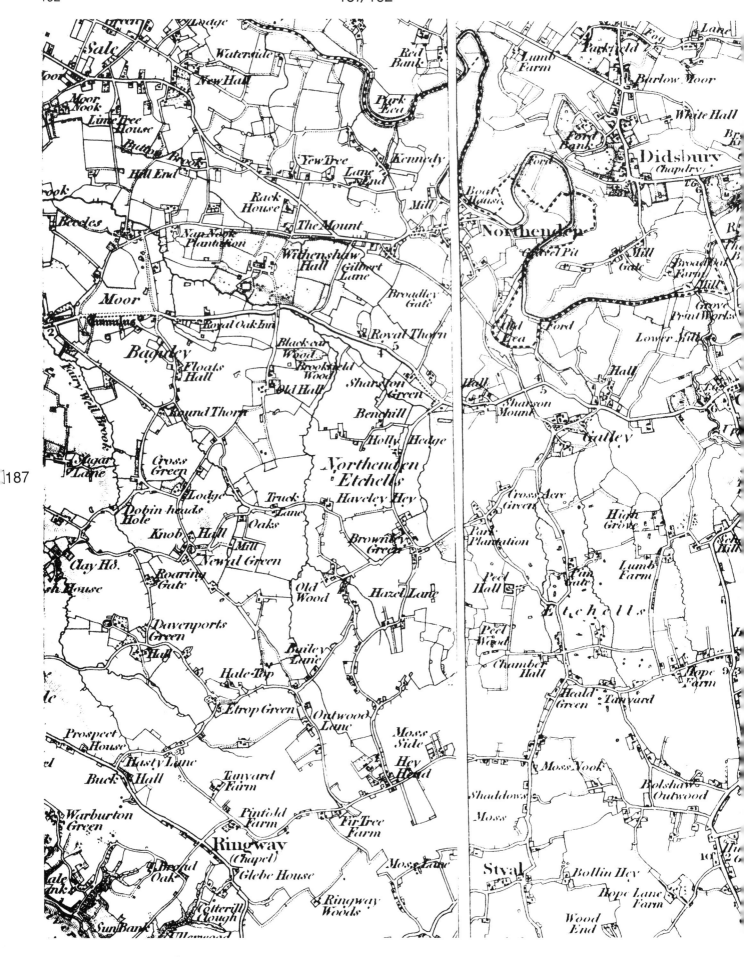

187

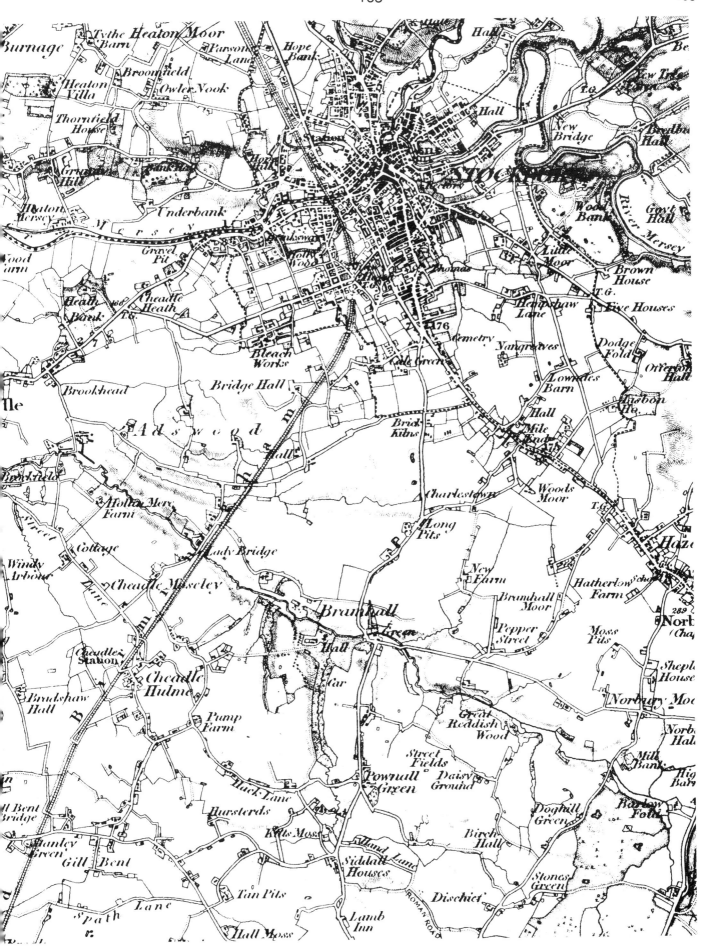

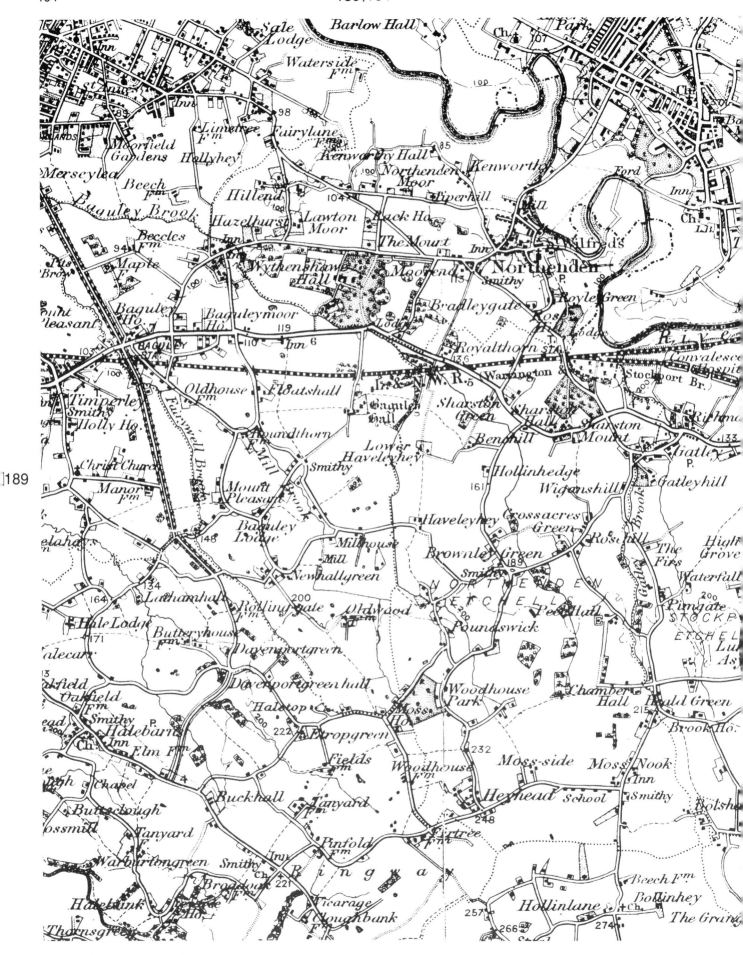

1 mile approx.

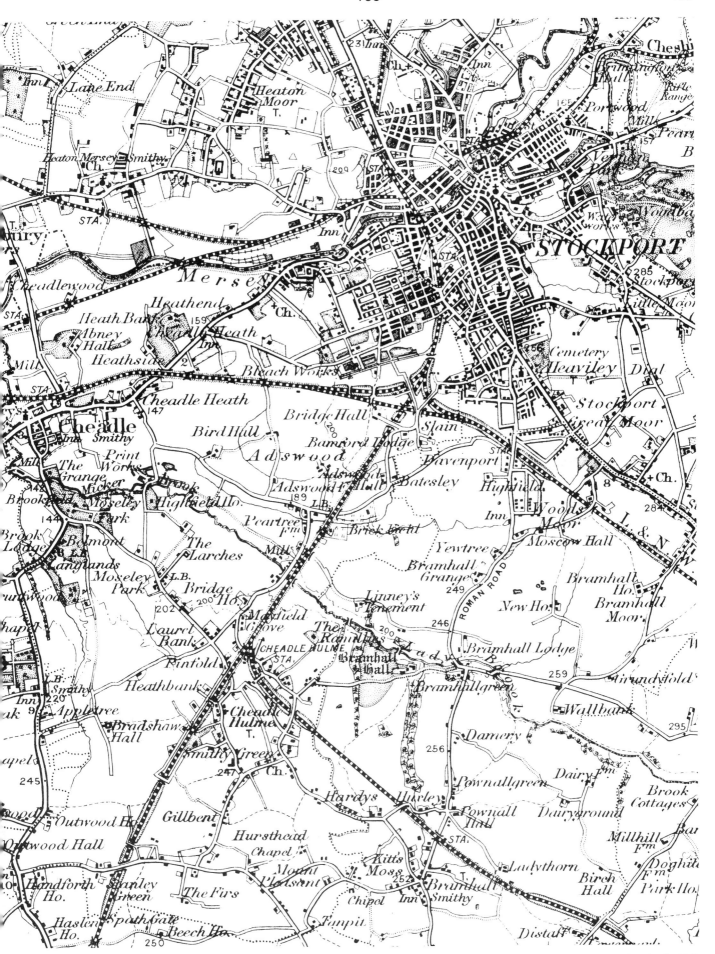

Surveyed 1870 - 75. Revised 1895. Published 1896.

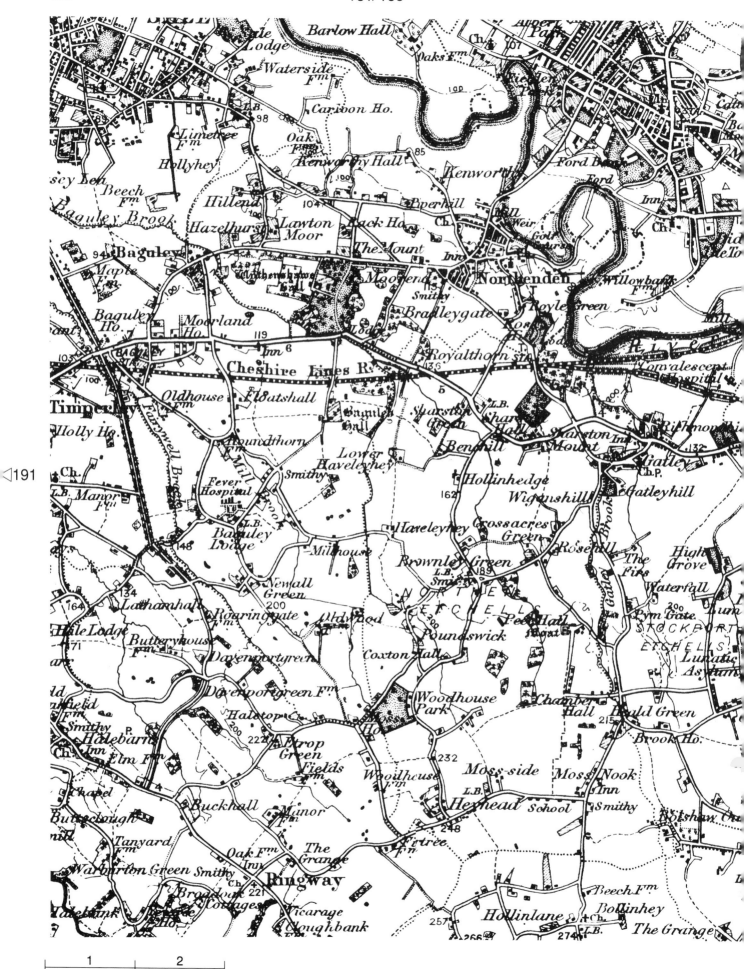

1 mile approx.

191

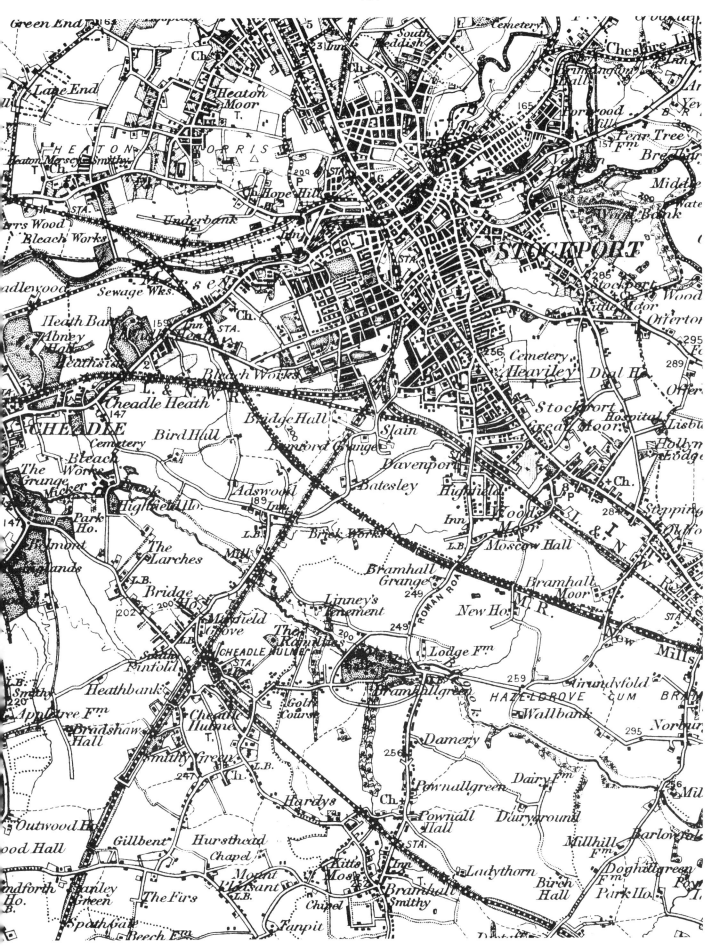

Surveyed 1870 - 75. Revised 1903. Published 1908.

1

2

1 mile approx.

New Snuggery

Little Crosby

Great Crosby

R.C. Chapel

Brighton

The

Crofton

H A R F

C r o s b y   C h a n n e l

C r o s

B A N K

U R B O

Published 1840 - 1844.

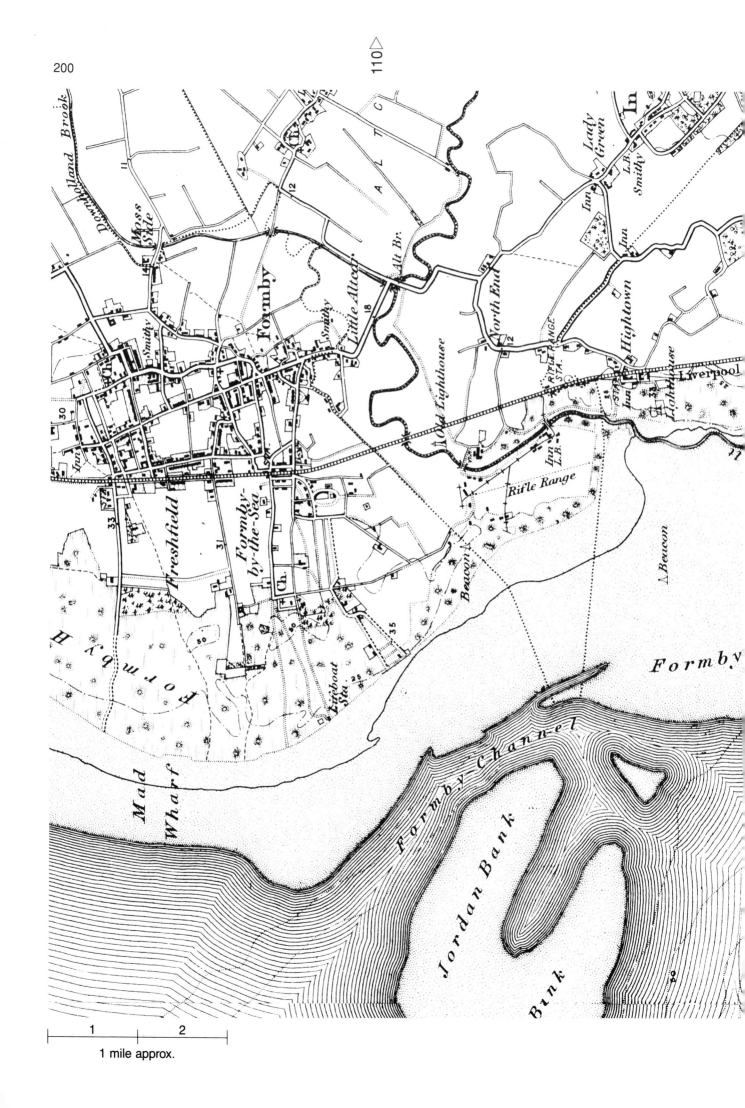

110△

Downholland Brook

Moss Side

A L T C

Lady Green

In

L.B.

Smithy

12

Alt Br.

Inn

Inn

Formby

Smithy

Little Altcar

18

North End

Inn

RIFLE RANGE

Hightown

Smithy

2

RIFLE STA.

Old Lighthouse

Inn

St.

Liverpool

Lighthouse

11

Freshfield

30

Inn

Formby-by-the-Sea

33

31

Ch.

35

Inn
L.B.

Rifle Range

Beacon

△Beacon

F o r m b y H

50

25

Beacon

Lifeboat Sta.

F o r m b y

Mad Wharf

F o r m b y   C h a n n e l

J o r d a n   B a n k

Bank

Bank

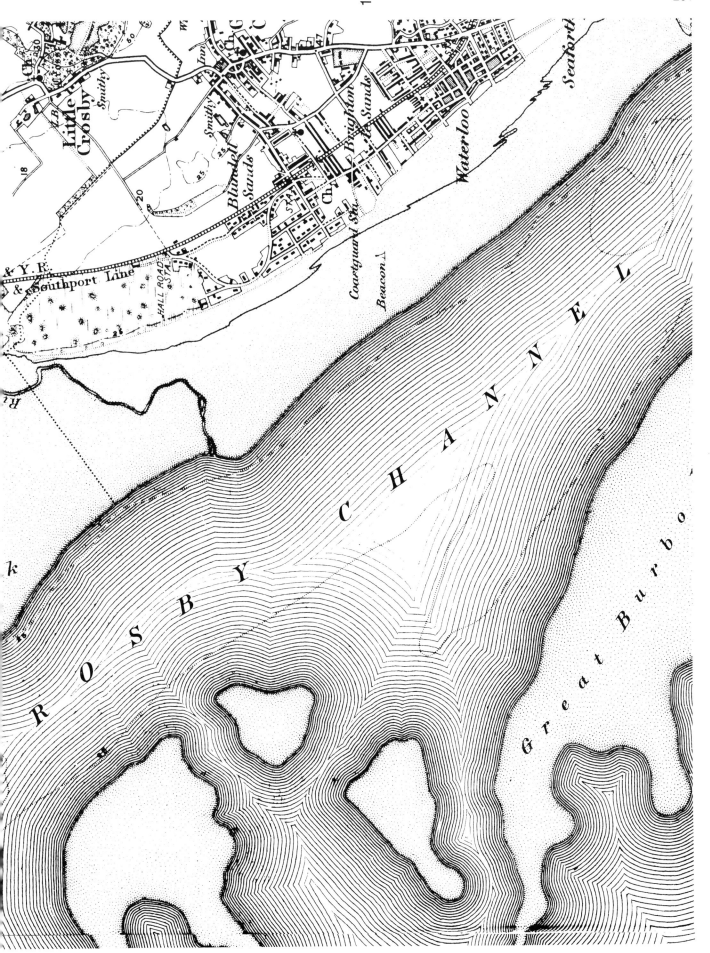

Surveyed 1869 - 74 / 1889 - 92. Revised 1892 - 95. Published 1896.

112 △

Downholland Brook

Moss Side

Formby Hall

A L T C

Alt Br.

Little Altcar

18

12

Formby

13

12

30

14

33

Freshfield

31

Raven Meols

35

Golf Links

Old Lighthouse

L.B.

Battery

Rifle Range

ALTCAR RIFLE RANGE

ALTCAR STA.

North End

Hightown

Inn

Smithy

Lady Green

10

Liverpool

Lifeboat Sta.

25

Mad Wharf

Formby Point

Formby Channel

25

Jordan Bank

Formby

Bank

Crosby Lightship

50

1   2

1 mile approx.

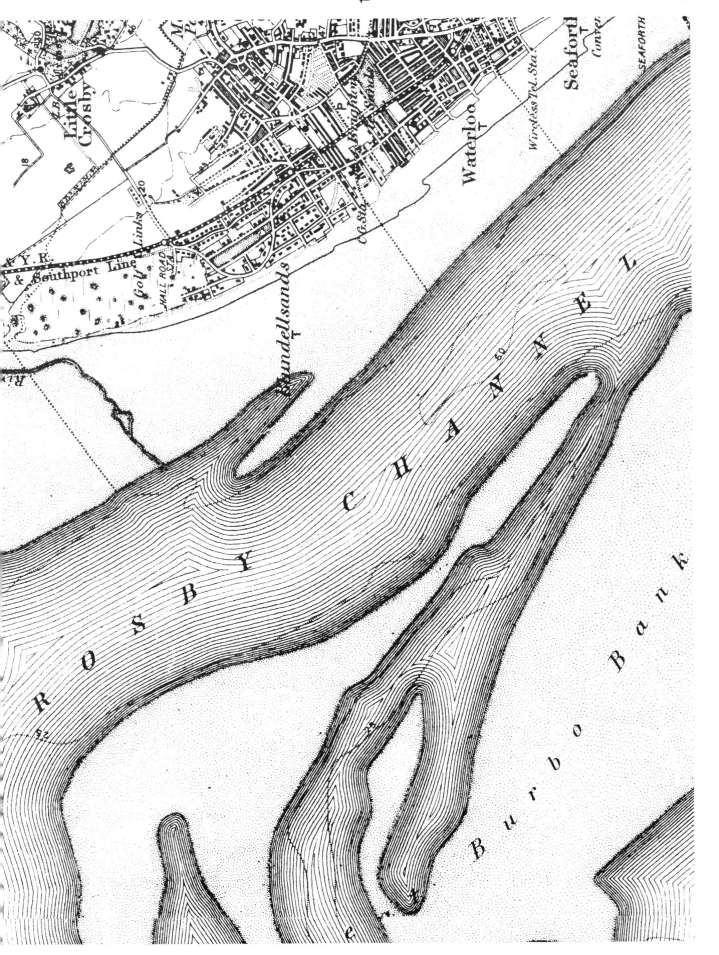

Surveyed 1843 - 49. Revised 1910. Published 1912.

Gazetteer

The following list of place names is not definitive; rather it is designed to stimulate the reader's interest and, used in conjunction with a modern day atlas, assists on a journey of discovering one's heritage.